MULTIMEDIA TOOLS AND APPLICATIONS

An International Journal

AF786284

Volume 4, No. 2, March 1997

Special Issue: Selected Papers from the 3rd IEEE International Workshop on Multimedia Database Management Systems
Guest Editors: Bhavani Thuraisingham, Kingsley C. Nwosu and P. Bruce Berra

ISBN 978-1-4613-7818-1 ISBN 978-1-4615-6149-1 (eBook)
DOI 10.1007/978-1-4615-6149-1

Library of Congress Cataloging-in-Publication Data

A C.I.P. Catalogue record for this book is available
from the Library of Congress.

Printed on acid-free paper.

Multimedia Tools and Applications, 4, 93–96 (1997)

Editorial

BHAVANI THURAISINGHAM thura@mitre.org
The MITRE Corp., Bedford, MA, USA.

KINGSLEY C. NWOSU nwosuck@harpo.wh.lucent.com
Lucent Technologies, Whippany, New Jersey, USA.

P. BRUCE BERRA berra@cat.syr.edu
CASE Center, Syracuse Univ., Syracuse, NY, USA.

A Multimedia Database Management System (MM-DBMS) should provide for the efficient storage and manipulation of data represented as text, images, voice, graphics, video, etc. In addition, users should also be able to periodically update the multimedia database so that information contained in it accurately reflects the real-world. Some MM-DBMSs have been extended to provide the capability of linking the various types of data in order to enable its users to have access to large amounts of related information within a short space of time either by browsing or querying the system. Recently a lot of research has been carried out on designing and developing MM-DBMSs, and, as a result, prototypes and commercial products are now available. However several areas are still under investigation - some of those areas are discussed below.

Data Model: Much of the earlier work on MM-DBMSs focussed on using an object-oriented data model for supporting different data types. However, several features such as synchronization mechanisms, relationships between the objects, decomposition and re-combination of objects need further research. Recently some conceptual models with some support for synchronization have been provided. In addition to developing a conceptual model for the representation of the objects, an appropriate specification language to specify the relationships and constraints needs to be developed. Finally, ways to integrate the constraint specification with the object specification needs to be examined so that impedance mismatch can be minimized.

Storage structures: While the data model describes the conceptual representation of the multimedia database, the storage structures describe the physical representation. That is, they are closer to the physical implementation of the database. Some efforts on storage management for multimedia databases (such as the use of clustering techniques) have been proposed. Mappings between the storage structures and the conceptual data model have to be provided. Special indexing techniques for multimedia databases need to be developed.

Architectures: Architectures will include system, schema, and functional architectures for the MM-DBMS. Various types of system architectures are possible. For example, in a distributed environment, one could assume that each database has its own data manager and these data managers are interconnected using some distributed processing module. In some cases, the local data managers may not exist and, therefore, the Distributed MM-DBMS will have to perform the functions of the local data managers. Schema architectures, such as the five-schema architecture, have been proposed for distributed database systems. The suitability of such architectures needs to be determined. Various data distribution schemes also need to be examined. For example, one scheme may not support the fragmentation of an object while another scheme may support it.

Retrieval Algorithms: Based on the the data model which will specify the operations on the objects, a retrieval language and, subsequently, the retrieval algorithms for each operation have to be designed. Support for content and context-based retrieval has to be examined. In addition, query transformation and optimization schemes have to be developed for each operation.

Update Algorithms: Update algorithms should handle replicated data, concurrent updates, and transaction processing. The notion of a transaction needs to be revisited for multimedia databases. In addition, techniques to support real-time constraints for transaction processing needs to be developed.

Meta-data Management: The types of meta-data for multimedia databases need to be identified. In many cases, the meta-databases may be quite large. Efficient techniques for storing, accessing, and maintaining meta-data need to be developed.

Multimedia database systems research is actively being pursued in several institutions and laboratories around the world. As a result, many of the major database management systems vendors are providing the capability to support multimedia data. To address some of the challenging issues for MM-DBMSs, the IEEE International workshop on MM-DBMS was founded. This special issue of the journal consists of the enhanced versions of some of the papers presented at the 3rd IEEE International workshop on MM-DBMS. This issue consists of six papers. The paper entitled: "Management of Multimedia Scenarios in an Object-Oriented Database System" by Djeraba, Hadouda, and Briand develops an object-oriented model to represent multimedia scenarious. The paper describes a temporal specification lanaguge and generates petrinets from the specification. Then the petrinets are used to detect errors and contradictions. The paper entitled: "The Architecture of the Dali Main-Memory Storage Manager" by Bohannon, Lieuwen, Rastogi, Silberschatz, Seshadri, and Sudarshan, describes the design of a main memory storage manager for multimedia databases. This storage manager supports both relational and object-oriented models and provides features such as indexing and concurrency control. The paper entitled: "Supporting Content-based Retrieval in Large Image Database Systems" by Remias, Sheikholeslami, Zhang, and Syeda-Mahmood describes retrieval techniques of image data by content. Modeling image data as well as query algorithms for image data are given. The paper entitled: "A Constraint-Driven Approach to Automate the Organization and Playout of Presentations in Multimedia Databases" by Hakkoymaz and Ozsoyoglu describes a constraint-driven methodolgy for presenting multimedia data. Constraints are used to extract semantics of multimedia segments. Playout algorithms are also described. The paper entitled: "Management of Multi-structured Hypermedia Documents: A Data Model, Query Language, and Indexing Scheme" by Lee, Lee, and Berra describes a structured approach to hypermedia document management. In particular, an object-oriented model query language, and retrieval techniques are proposed. Finally, the paper entitled: "Techniques for Fast Partitioning of Compressed and Uncompressed Video" by Adjeroh, Lee, and Orji describes video partitioning, and the techniques used to represent identifiable scenes in a video script. Formal methods are utilized to ensure that decisions on similar scenes are made reliably.

The six papers described in this special issue will address some of the challenges identified. These include data modeling, architecture, and query language and processing issues. We believe that the reader will benefit from the contents of this special issue.

Dr. Bhavani Thuraisingham is a Senior Principal Engineer with the MITRE Corporation's National Intelligence Division, and is a strategic technology area leader in the Advanced Information Systems Center where she heads the data and information management section. She also heads the Corporate Initiative on Evolvable Interoperable Information Systems. She is currently working on real-time database management for command and control applications, massive multimedia database management for intelligence applications, data mining/knowledge discovery related to data security, and distributed object management technology. She is also a Co-Director of MITRE's Database Specialty Group. Prior to joining MITRE, Dr. Thuraisingham was with Honeywell Inc. and before that at Control Data Corporation. She was also an adjunct professor of computer science and a member of the graduate faculty at the University of Minnesota. Dr. Thuraisingham has published over two hundred and fifty technical papers and reports including over forty journal articles, and holds two U.S. patents for MITRE on database inference control. She has been a featured speaker at several conferences including Object World West '95 and '96, Object World East '96, IFIP Database Security Conference '96, and the DoD Database Colloquium '94, '95, and 96. Dr. Thuraisingham has an M.S. degree in Computer Science from the University of Minnesota, an M.Sc degree in Mathematical Logic from the University of Bristol, U.K,. and a Ph.D. degree in Computability Theory from the University of Wales, Swansea, U.K. She is a member of ACM, IEEE Computer Society, the British Computer Society, and AFCEA.

Kingsley C. Nwosu is a Member of Technical Staff with Lucent Technologies, Whippany, New Jersey. He is also a Adjunct Professor in the Department of Mathematics and Computer Science, Rutgers University, Newark; a visiting Professor in the Department of Mathematics and Computer Science, Montclair State University; and an Adjunct Professor in the Computer Science Department at College of Saint Elizabeth, Madison, New Jersey.

Before joining Lucent Technologies, he was a Research Staff Member with IBM in Kingston, New York, where he was involved in High Performance File System design and development.
Dr. Nwosu is very active in the area of multimedia systems research and development having published several papers in this area and served in several conferences/workshops.
Dr. Nwosu holds an M.S. degree in Computer Science from the University of Southwestern Louisiana, Lafayette, Louisiana, an M.S. in Computer Science from the Univeristy of Oklahoma, Norman, Oklahoma, and a Ph.D. in Computer Science from Syracuse University, Syracuse, New York. His current areas of research include Multimedia Information/Computing Systems, Object-Oriented Programming/Design, Distributed Processing/Computing, Information Storage/Retrieval, and Parallel Algorithm Design and Analysis.
He is an active member of ACM, IEEE Computer and Communications Societies, New York Academy of Science, National Council on Systems Engineering, and Mathematical Association of America.

P. Bruce Berra. See paper titled "Management of Multi-structured Hypermedia Documents: A Data Model, Query Language, and Indexing Scheme."

Multimedia Tools and Applications, 4, 97–114 (1997)

Management of Multimedia Scenarios in an Object-Oriented Database System

CHABANE DJERABA, KARIMA HADOUDA, HENRI BRIAND cdjeraba@ireste.fr
IRIN, IRESTE, Nantes University, La Chantrerie, CP 3003, 44087 Nantes cedex 03, France

Abstract. In this paper, we present an approach to multimedia scenario management in a database system that considers : object-oriented concepts for multimedia and scenario modeling; both known and unknown multimedia object playing duration; temporal specification language; Petri net automatic generation based on temporal specifications; automatic detection of user temporal specification errors and contradictions; and finally user interactions based on composite Petri net features.

Keywords: Multimedia, temporal relations, interactions, Petri net, object-oriented concepts, database

1. Introduction

The management of scenarios is a significant part of multimedia databases. Scenarios are natural means of playing and modeling temporal composition relations between media in an application domain; that is why, multimedia database has to manage temporal compositions which consist in presenting multimedia objects, using synchronization among different media.

Our approach defines a domain expert useful environment for scenario generations. The scenario generation is composed of three important stages:

- An user temporal specification based on an appropriate temporal specification language, which is itself based on both extensions of Allen's temporal relations [3] and time interval- model.
- An automatic generation of a Petri net based on the previous temporal specification. The Petri net is stored in an object called *scenario object.*
- Finally, an interpretation or a simulation of the scenario object which leads to scenario presentations with domain expert interactions.

Our approach, based on object concepts, models media and scenario objects, their properties and operations. This gives a set of building blocks, known as classes, that can be incorporated into an Object-Oriented DataBase Management System (OODBMS).

In this paper, we highlight the following points : scenario temporal specification (section 2), temporal Petri net generation (section 3), interactions with the domain expert (section 4), object-oriented modeling in an OODBMS (section 5), and a simple example that illustrates our approach (section 6).

2. Scenario Temporal Specifications

Many existing specification models of multimedia temporal composition are based on Allen's relations. However, the current implementations of Allen's relations are not appropriate enough for some real world temporal compositions. The multimedia object duration must be known before designing the scenario, and any change in the duration may modify the temporal relations that exist between the multimedia objects. We propose a temporal composition model based on an optional temporal duration. In our temporal specification, the user has the possibility to define a temporal specification which may be either relations depending on multimedia object duration or relations reflecting causal dependencies between multimedia objects when the duration is unknown.

2.1. Related works

Multimedia temporal models may be decomposed into two categories : instant-based and interval-based [19]. Several approaches support instant-based models such as Hy-Time [11], temporal point nets [4], MME [6], [8]. In instant based models, each event, such as the start or the end of the media, has its time instant, so all the events are ordered on the time line. Although the models are quite appropriate for temporal synchronization among determined duration media, they are not appropriate for undetermined duration media. Their creation and updating may result in very complex graphs, and may generate inconsistent specifications, in which case a complex verification process has to be designed to control inconsistencies.

In interval-based models, the basic media units are time intervals which represent multimedia object durations. The intervals are, generally ordered, according to Allen's relations [3] *(before, meet, overlap, finish, during, start, equal)*. Many approaches are based on Allen's relations. For example, [13] proposes an OCPN model equivalent to Allen's relations. [12] develops a temporal specification based on a temporal logic. He describes Allen's relations by using temporal logic model based on mathematical concepts. This model is mathematically powerful, but it is not simple to use by designers. Furtheremore, the model requires methods to verify consistency and to execute a given temporal specification.

Most interval-based models face some disadvantages. Firstly, the temporal relations are designed to specify relations between multimedia objects of determined duration, but they are not designed to specify relations that are not explicitly determined by the user. So, the majority of current models are interesting for describing presentations in which all start and end instants of multimedia objects are determined and fixed, but they are not appropriate when the duration of multimedia objects is not fixed. Secondly, the detection of inconsistent specifications, that may be introduced into a multimedia presentation, requires a complex process. In order to resolve these disadvantages, a recent approach [20], considered in some systems such as [7] and [1], is proposed to allow causal relations between multimedia objects of unknown duration. It defines a set of operators expressing causal relations between multimedia objects. It can be used to form nested multimedia object expressions. Multimedia object expressions are independent of multimedia object durations, and allow encapsulation and structured nesting. It proposes six temporal and causal composition operators : *seq, par, start, par-min, par-max, ident, equal*. *x seq y* defines a composition in which the end of the multimedia object x starts the multimedia object y. *x par y* defines a composition in which the beginning of the multimedia object x starts the multimedia object y. *x par-min y* defines a composition in which the beginning of the multimedia object x starts the multimedia object y. The resulting multimedia object is stopped when the latter of the two multimedia objects is terminated. *x par-max y* defines a composition in which the beginning of the multimedia object x starts the multimedia object y. The resulting multimedia object is stopped when the latter of the two multimedia objects is terminated. *x equal y* defines a composition in which the multimedia object x starts and stops the multimedia object y. *x ident y* defines a composition in which the beginning of the multimedia object x starts y, and the end of the multimedia object y stops x. One disadvantage of this approach is that not all temporal compositions can be described [7]. For example, the temporal compositions that contain interleaved start and stop actions on parallel branches cannot be described. Another disadvantage of this approach is its dependency aspects. It allows the expression of causal relations between multimedia objects. So, if a multimedia object fails, all the multimedia objects that depend of the failed multimedia object fail too. In the interval-based model, the consequences of the failed multimedia object are limited to this multimedia object during the duration associated to it.

2.1.1. *Our scenario temporal specification*

We will present a model for temporal composition of multimedia objects. The model is based on time-interval and differs from earlier works in one major aspect. We consider the seven relations of Allen *(equal, meet, finish, start, before, overlap, during)* with the following feature: multimedia object expressions may be dependent of the duration, for a known duration, or independent of the duration, for an unknown duration. In this case, the event of the end of the multimedia object is detected by the system that supports the synchronization mechanism when the presentation of the multimedia object is finished, and the system associates the duration resulting from the execution of the multimedia object with the previous multimedia object.

Our basic unit is the time interval associated with multimedia objects. The time interval of the multimedia object x may be defined by the end and start instants.

$(x.start \leq x.end)$ *and* $x = (t \,/\, x.start \leq t \leq x.end)$

The duration of the multimedia object *x* is equal to *x.start - x.end* (e.g. t = 10 minutes). It is dependent on the playing time of the multimedia object (e.g. playing time of an audio object) if it is known, but it takes into account the unknown multimedia object duration (e.g. the duration is not determined by the user).

Each program of our specification language for the temporal composition is divided into three parts : declaration, assign and temporal relations. The declaration part contains the declarations of multimedia objects.

multimedia-object (duration) : Type

The duration is optional for continuous media such as video and audio, but obligatory for non-continuous media such as images. For example:

video : VIDEO

video1 (15) : VIDEO

image1 (20) : IMAGE

The assign part contains the assign functions between the objects declared in the first part and the data streams. For example, the data streams may be mpeg or jpeg files, for example:

assign (video1, " file1.mpeg ")

assign (image1, " file2.jpeg ")

When using several equal multimedia objects of the same media, we have to declare several multimedia objects with the same duration assigned to the same physical support. For example, if video3 and video4 share the same physical object with the same duration, we will have :

video3 (duration1) : VIDEO

video4 (duration1) : VIDEO

assign (video3, " file3.mpeg ")

assign (video4, " file3.mpeg ")

When using several multimedia objects of the same media with different duration, we have to declare several multimedia objects with different duration assigned to the same physical support. For example, if *video3* and *video4* share the same physical object with different duration, we will have:

video3 (duration1) : VIDEO

video4 (duration2) : VIDEO

assign (video3, " file3.mpeg ")

assign (video4, " file3.mpeg ")

The temporal relation part, contains a set of functions or procedures, each one representing a binary Allen's relation between multimedia objects of known or unknown duration. These multimedia objects are either declared objects and assigned to physical supports, or objects resulting from temporal relations. A relation takes two multimedia objects as arguments and returns a multimedia object as a result:

multimedia object3 = temporal-relation (multimedia object1, multimedia object2)

The resulting multimedia object may be used as an argument of another temporal relation. Example of relations:

(equal(starts(meets (video1, video2), meet (text1, text2)),image1)

or

multimedia-object1 := meets(video1, video2)

multimedia-object2 := meets(text1, text2)

multimedia-object3 := starts(multimedia-object1, multimedia-object2)

equals(multimedia-object3, image1)

Before the generation of the Petri net, the language will verify the temporal consistency by detecting the user's temporal specification errors such as contradictions between temporal relations and duration of the user's program, for example:

- x equal y, but x.duration is not equal to y.duration.
- x overlap y with d.delay, but d.delay + x.duration is less than or equal to y.duration, or d.delay is greater than y.duration.
- x during y with d.delay, but d.delay + x.duration is greater than or equal to y.duration.
- x finish y with d.delay, but d.delay + x.duration is not equal to y.duration.

3. Temporal Petri net generation

Our Petri net may be considered as a variant of the temporal Petri net developed in several works [13], [12], [16] with these interesting features:

1. The Petri net is generated automatically on the basis of the user's temporal specifications that help him to define temporal relations naturally and simply without any considerations of Petri net details.

2. The Petri net considers multimedia objects of known or unknown duration, and after each execution, the language associates the duration with the multimedia objects whose duration were unknown before the execution. So, the Petri net corrects itself.

3. Thirdly, during the generation of the Petri net on the basis of the temporal specification, the language detects contradictions between temporal relations. This automatic detection helps the user to improve his temporal specification. For example, when two multimedia objects are declared with different duration, and linked by equal temporal relation, then the system returns a specification error. Let us consider the following temporal relation:

   multimedia-object1 (20) : VIDEO

   multimedia-object2 (30) : VIDEO

   equal (multimedia-object1, multimedia-object2)

   In this example, equal temporal relation is not respected, because the two multimedia objects have different duration.

4. After the generation of the Peti net, the system returns, when requested by the user, the simulation of the scenario that corresponds to the Petri net generated. This simulation may detect two kinds of errors: graph design errors (i.e. a multimedia object that is declared but never used) and allocation resource errors (i.e. allocation of the same resource to several multimedia objects, it is the classical problem of mutual exclusion on a critical resource).

Based on the user's temporal specification, our language generates a Petri net automatically and stores the Petri net generated in a scenario object (section 5). Each temporal relation is associated with a temporal Petri net, as illustrated by [9], and modeled in several approaches, such as in OCPN of [13]. This mapping is helpful for an automatic generation of a temporal Petri net. Let us consider $T\alpha$, $T\beta$, $T\gamma$ that model respectively the duration of places $P\alpha$, $P\beta$ and $P\gamma$. Each Petri net, associated with a temporal relation, has to respect the temporal constraint associated with it. For example, the Petri net associated with the *start* temporal relation has to respect the temporal constraint $T\alpha \leq T\beta$. In this way, the system can differentiate between *start* and *equal* temporal relations, and between *during*, *overlap* and *finish* temporal relations.

Our Petri net is a 7-tuple one, defined as follows: P = (T, P, A, M, R, O, D).

- T = (t1, t2, ..) is a finite set of transitions.
- P = (p1, p2, ..) is a finite set of places. A place represents the *play* process of a multimedia object.

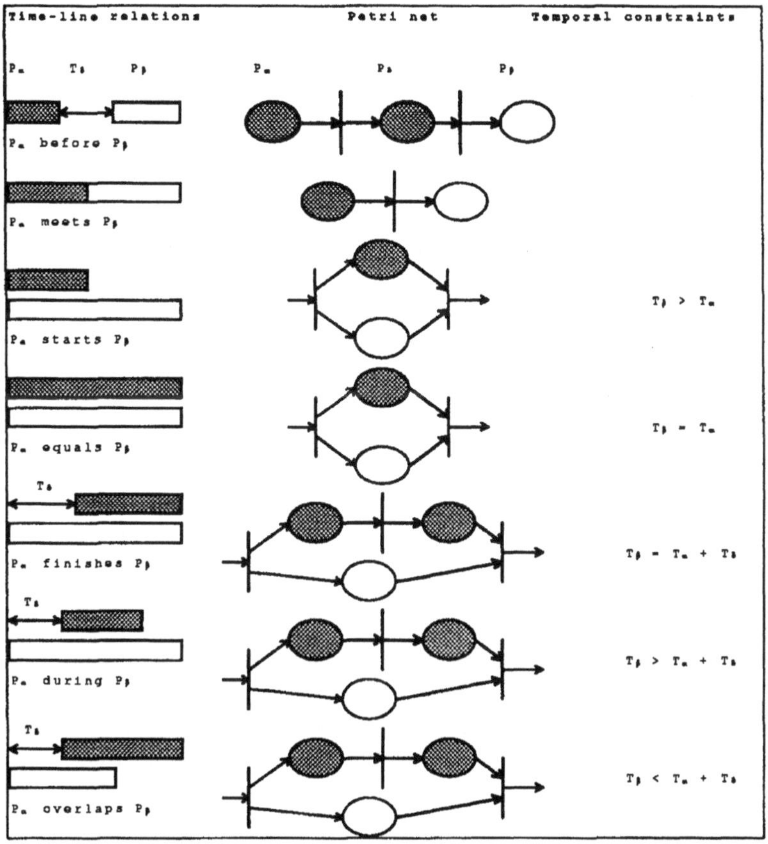

Figure 1. Petri nets and temporal constraints associated with temporal relations.

- A : (PxT) or (TxP) —— N is a mapping from a set of places and transitions to the integer numbers, and represents values of arcs. Each arc models a flow relation. The arc values are generally equal to 1 or -1.

- M : P —— N is a mapping from a place to the number of tokens in the place. The cardinal of place tokens is generally less or equal to 1.

- R : P —— Res is a mapping from a set of places to the resources needed.

- D: P —— Time is a mapping from the set of places to the integer number representing the amount of time consumed.

- O : P —– (Multimedia-objects x Time) is a mapping from the set of places to a set of multimedia objects and their duration.

Each place is assigned a duration corresponding to the multimedia object. A time function, associated with each place, models the time consumed (c_t) at any given time. When all

Table 1. Some rules.

1. If $c_t = 0$ then the execution of the multimedia object has not been started.
2. When entering a place, a token is first locked, it indicates that the multimedia object is being executed, so: $0 \leq c_t \leq multimedia.object.duration$.
3. IF the play process is finished, the token is unlocked, $multimedia.object.duration \leq c_t$.
4. If $c_t > multimedia.object.duration$, it means that the multimedia object is waiting to be synchronized with some other multimedia objects.

input places of a transition have unlocked tokens, then the tokens are consumed and the transition fires. So, each output place of the transition will receive a token. A token place becomes ready to enable a transition after the end of the duration associated with this place, starting from the time the place receives the token. The places in our temporal Petri net are also used to represent delays which may be needed to support the various forms of temporal relations that may exist between multimedia objects.

There are several advantages in the generation of a Petri net : Firstly, the language that supports the Petri net verifies that there are no resource allocation errors. For example, the language verifies that the same hardware necessary to execute an audio stream is not allocated to two multimedia objects that should be executed in the same time. Secondly, the domain expert has the possibility to request the graphical simulation of scenarios before the execution of the Petri net. Thirdly, after one execution of the Petri net, the language updates the previously unknown duration of multimedia objects. If the user changes the duration, the language automatically generates another Petri net which respects the principles that have already been presented. This is an interesting feature of our language, because there is no need to modify the temporal Petri net directly. After duration modifications, the language generates automatically the appropriate temporal Petri net, if it does not detect temporal specification inconsistencies.

In our approach, all scenarios can be expressed and executed by using our specification language, but there is a price to pay for the automatic generation of the Petri net from the temporal specification. The language verifies that there are no contradictions between temporal relations, between temporal relations and duration, and verifies that there are no inconsistencies in the Petri net. This operation is time-consuming when the Petri net is complicated. some authors, such as [7], say that the resulting graph becomes complicated and difficult to manipulate and to modify. In our approach, the modification is very simple, because it does not concern the Petri net, but the temporal specification which is natural and simple to use.

4. User Interactions

Our approach synchronizes the scenario with the user (i.e domain expert). The interaction takes the form of pausing, resuming, reversing, forwarding and browsing through objects.

User interactions can be classified into two classes: basic interactions and general interactions. Basic interactions concern user elementary operations such as *pause, resume*, reverse and forward. In *pause, resume* operations, the system records the current temporal image of the scenario modeled by a Petri net, and when resume operation is executed, the system loads the amount of time that the scenario had paused, and the presentation starts again from where it stopped.

The reverse operation is specified in terms of temporal skip given by the user. Example *(goes back 15 minutes)*. When the reverse operation is requested, the Petri net deals with objects associated with places currently being presented. So, the system determines the new consumption time for all the places of the objects that are in a parallel temporal execution. Let us consider : pi a place, and tpi an input transition to pi. The system modifies the consumption time for the input places of the transition. There are reverse fires of the transition tpi, and also input transitions to other objects in parallel relations with it, and thus the execution of multimedia objects starts again. Upon restarting, the consumption of objects is advanced to new values. If the reverse operation involves objects that are further behind pi in the presentation graph, the presentation graph is traversed backwards until the target object is reached. However, for each intermediate transition between the target and pi, the consumption time for its input places is set to zero, indicating that the object represented in such places can still consume time.

The *forward* operation is similar to the reverse operation with this difference: *forward* is not possible if the internal duration is unknown. If the system meets an object with an unknown duration, the forward operation will fail.

In general interactions, our approach is similar to [2], the user branches out of the current scenario, so he effectively modifies the current scenario. Let us consider a multimedia database representing scenes of a visitor in an art gallery. The highlight on a spatial art object is possible through animation. When the database contains images of all possible art objects, visiting may include highlight and corresponding jumps out of the sequential nature of the sequence of images corresponding to art objects. To approach this problem, we use the hierarchical modeling capability of the Petri net scenario. A place can be another temporal Petri net. So, there is a global Petri net that is composed of sub-nets of smaller Petri nets corresponding to scenarios. Branching to different scenario graph is then equivalent to following a hypermedia relation, so the user can select a branch to any part of the global scenario, or follow the scenario schedule as previously defined in the current global scenario.

At each branching point, our approach models a hypermedia node. Before the branch scenario is chosen, the hypermedia node appears as a hypermedia button, with an internal duration independent of the multimedia object duration of the button. So, if the branch is not selected by the user, the scenario represented by the sub-net will not be presented, and the Petri net associated with it will not be executed.

B1 : *BUTTON*

VIDEO1 *(20) : VIDEO*

INTERACTION *(b1, video1)*

SCENARIO1 : *SCENARIO*

INTERACTION *(b1, scenario1)*

When selecting the button, the user branches to another scenario, the sub-net representing the new scenario is considered as the current scenario. If the user does not branch (there is no selection of the button) to another scenario associated with the button, the button is presented without any consideration of the presentation sub-net associated with it. After the sub-net execution is finished, the presentation goes back to the composite net. Continuation of the former presentation graph is achieved by using its pre-recorded state in the same manner as a *pause/resume* operation. With this approach, a sub-net corresponding to a presentation can be integrated to any node. A sub-net may be composed of other sub-nets depending on the application area.

Other approaches have been implemented for interactive movies by using the hypertext paradigm [5]. A hypertext called Petri-Net-Based-Hypertext (PNBH) [18] describes data units as net places and links as net arcs. Transitions in PNBH indicate the transversal relations.

5. Object-Oriented Modeling

Our multimedia framework looks to the framework proposed in [8]. It is composed of abstract classes serving to specify interfaces, and suggested procedures for using the classes. The abstract classes are specialized for different multimedia platforms. So, applications using the abstract classes may adapt to variations in platform functionality.

The classes of our framework belong to two distinct groups : media classes and scenario classes. Media classes correspond to audio, video, image, text, and other media types, their basic properties and operations, and scenario classes model temporal composition of media objects. In this paper, we will focus on scenario classes which is a main difference with the framework presented in [8].

Scenarios are divided into types corresponding to application domains. Each type is represented by a class. These are called scenario classes and form a hierarchy. Nodes depict classes and edges depict superclass/subclass relationships. An edge points from the superclass to the subclass. Instances of scenario classes are called scenario objects. A scenario class models scenario object properties and operations.

5.1. Scenario object properties

The properties of the scenario object consist of an internal representation of the Petri net, descriptors and an attribute that points to the root of the temporal composition hierarchy.

The internal representation of the Petri net consists of:

- A dynamic array in which each ith element contains the number of tokens associated with the ith place.
- A matrix in which each line l represents a transition, and each column c represents a place, and an element of the $matrix(l, c)$ represents the value of the arc between l^{th} transition and c^{th} place. This number is positive when the arc is situated before the transition, and negative when the arc is situated after the transition. Generally, the values are equal to $+1$ or -1. When there is no flow relation between the place l and the transition c, then $matrix(l, c) = 0$.
- A dynamic array that represents duration and multimedia object identifiers associated with places. Each ith element of the array contains the duration and the multimedia object identifier of the ith place.
- A dynamic array that represents the resources allocated to each place.
- And other arrays [17].

Descriptors bundle together attributes of scenario objects such as their global size, date of generation, comments and name, while the root of the temporal composition hierarchy corresponds to a root of binary tree indicating pairs of entities with associated temporal intervals. For this tree, we allow three node types, terminal, non terminal and root.

Table 2. Scenario and Tree class.

- ***Class Scenario*** inherit Object read type
  tuple (indicematrix : Matrix, resourcevector : vector, durationvector : vector, tokenvector : vector, descriptor : Descriptor, root: Tree) method public generate (filename : string) : boolean, public delete, public simulate, public interpret
  end;
- ***Class Tree*** inherit Object read type
- tuple (temporalrelation : relation, leftentity : Tree, rightentity : Tree, delay : integer, nodetype : string, duration : integer, mediaobject : Media)
  end;

A terminal node type has attributes that indicate the node type (terminal, non terminal, root), the media object identifier, and the media object duration. Nonterminal nodes include the node type, left and right child entities and the temporal relation.

An interesting point here is the existence of two equivalent representations of the same scenario. The first one corresponds to the internal representation of the Petri net associated to the scenario. This internal representation is necessary for both simulation and interpretation of the scenario. The second one corresponds to the temporal composition hierarchy whose root is pointed by the attribute *root*. The temporal composition hierarchy is a binary tree of the scenario that may be useful to support retrieve scenarios when specifying the content represented by descriptors.

5.2. *Scenario object operations*

The methods of the scenario class are divided into two categories: *generation, deletion* and *simulation, interpretation*. The generation method allows applications to generate scenario objects using temporal specifications.

Scenario s;

s - generate (" file ");

.............;

s - delete;

The method *simulate* simulates graphically the scenario using the Petri net associated to the scenario object.

Scenario s;

s - generate (" file ");

s - simulate ;

The method *interpret* plays the scenario.

s - interpret;

It returns the scenario by playing media objects included in the scenario with respect of the temporal constraints that characterize the scenario.

6. Example

This example will illustrate some notions presented above. The scenario is composed of a video object that describes the different members of the Simpson family (Homer, Bart, Maggie, Lisa and Marge). Each appearance of a member of the family in the video object triggers an image and a text of that member.

The temporal specification associated to this scenario is stored by the user in a file named *simpsons.scenario*.

Table 3. Temporal Specification program of the scenario: "simpsons.scenario"

- ***scenario*** Simpsons
- ***declarations***
  TexteBart (90) : TEXTE; ImageBart(90) : IMAGE; TexteHomer (90) : TEXTE; ImageHomer(90) : IMAGE; TexteMaggie (180) : TEXTE; ImageMaggie(180) : IMAGE; TexteMarge (110) : TEXTE; ImageMarge(110) : IMAGE; TexteLisa (100) : TEXTE; ImageLisa(100) : IMAGE; AudioSimpson (900) : AUDIO; VideoSimpsons (900) : VIDEO;
- ***assigns***
  assign(VideoSimpsons, simpsonsv.mpg); assign(AudioSimpson, simpsonsa.mpg); assign(TexteBart, bart.txt); assign(ImageBart, bart.gif); ......
- ***relations***
  VarBart := equal (ImageBart, TexteBart); VarHomer := equal (ImageHomer, TexteHomer); arVideoAudioSimpsons := equal (VideoSimpsons, AudioSimpsons); ....

  during(before (before(VarBart, VarHomer,20) overlaps (finishes(VarMarge, VarMaggie, 70) Lisa, 55),),20),VarVideoAudioSimpsons,100);
- fin.

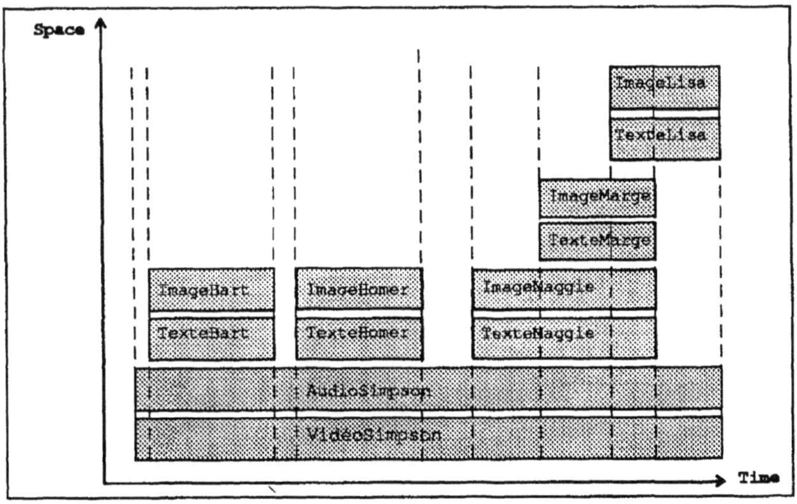

Figure 2. Time line diagram of the scenario.

Scenario SimpsonsScenario;

SimpsonsScenario - generate (" simpsons.scenario ");

SimpsonsScenario, instance of the class *scenario*, is generated and updated.

When the user requests the simulation of the scenario *SimpsonsScenario - simulate*, the system returns the simulation of the Petri net.

When the user requests the execution of the scenario, *SimpsonsScenario - interpret*, the system plays the scenario.

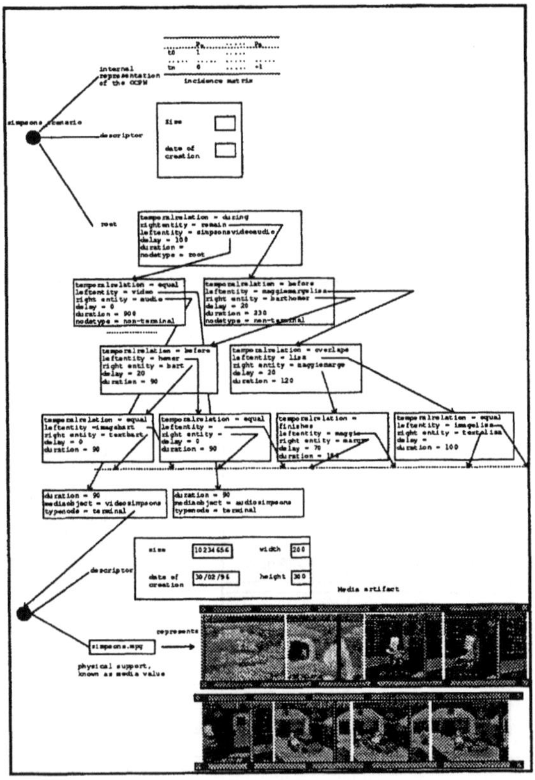

Figure 3. SimpsonsScenario object.

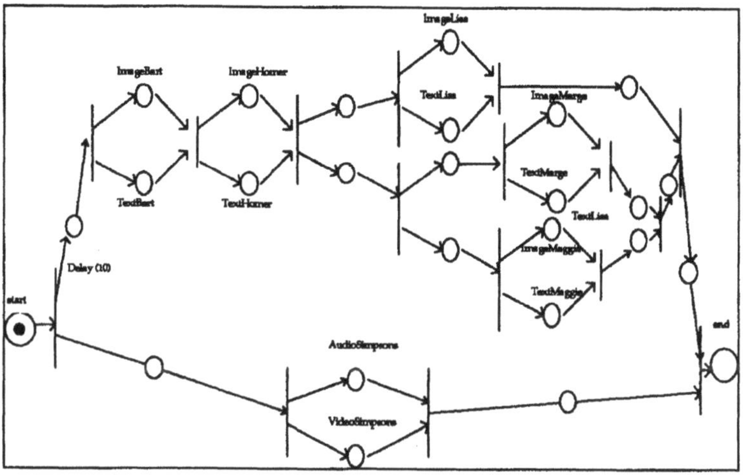

Figure 4. SimpsonsScenario simulation.

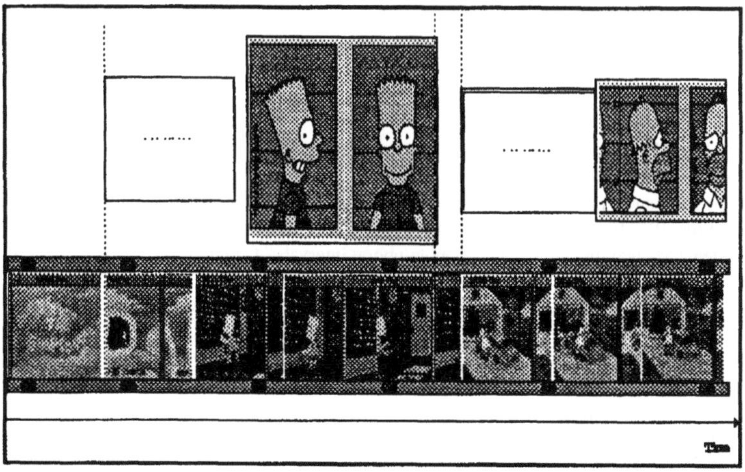

Figure 5. A part of SimpsonsScenario interpretation.

7. Conclusion

We have presented a language for multimedia scenario generation. Our language features consider : -both known and unknown duration, -temporal specification language, -Petri net automatic generation, -automatic detection of user temporal specification errors and contradictions, - and finally user interactions based on composite temporal Petri net.

The system is implemented on IBM Risc 6000/Aix platform using the programming language C++. The current version of the object-oriented database O2 supports features which can integrate C++ libraries; this makes the current integration of the C++ modules of our language easy and safe. The database also supports the data structures, but multimedia data are stored in files. Continuous media data are stored in mpeg files, while non continuous media data are stored in gif and jpeg files.

In the future, we will perform the algorithms that detect inconsistencies in the temporal Petri net generated, and we will provide a support for the programmer to develop distributed multimedia applications using the object-oriented model. It is important to provide the communication of various types of data over the high speed ATM network and the synchronization of the multimedia objects at the target system. The target system is the location in which the final synchronization is executed respecting the network delay with insignificant modifications of the earlier synchronization.

Acknowledgments

We would like to thank Fouad MAAREF, Luc MILLET, Vincent STEPHANE and Helene VILLAUME for many interesting suggestions.

References

1. M. Adiba, "STORM, Structural and Temporal Object-oRiented Multimedia database system," Proc. IW-MDBMS-95, Newark, August 1995, pp. 12–19.
2. D.A. Adjeroh and M.C. Lee, "Synchronisation Mechanisms for Distributed Multimedia Presentation Systems," Proc. IW-MDBMS-95, Newark, August 1995, pp. 30–37.
3. J.F. Allen, "Maintaining knowledge about temporal intervals," Commun. ACM, vol. 26, no. 11, November 1983, pp. 832–843.
4. M.C. Buchanan, Zellweger P., T., "Automatic Temporal Layout Mechanisms," Proc. ACM Multimedia 1993, Anaheim, CA, August 1993, pp. 341–350.
5. J. Conklin, "Hypertext: An introduction and Survey," Computer, pp. 17-41, Sep. 1987, pp. 17–41.
6. D. Dingeldein, "Modeling multimedia objects with MME," Proc. Eurographics Workshop on Object-Oriented Graphics, Sintra, Portugal, May 1994.
7. A. Duda and C. Keramane, "Structural Temporal Composition of Multimedia Data," Proc. IW-MMDBMS-95, Newark, August 1995, pp. 136-142.
8. S. Gibbs, C. Breiteneder, and D. Tsichritzis, "Audio/Video Databases: An Object- Oriented Approach," Proc. IEEE Ninth International Conference on Data Engineering, Vienna, April 1993.
9. C.L. Hamblin, "Instants and intervals," Proc. 1st Int. Conf. Soc. For the Study Time, Spring-Verlag, 1972, pp. 324-331.
10. N. Hirzalla and A. Karmouch, "Multimedia Content Retrieval System," Technical report, Electrical Eng. Dept., University of Ottawa, Nov. 1994.

11. "Information technology hypermedia/time-based structuring language (HyTime)," ISO International Standard, (ISO/IEC IS 10744), August 1992.
12. P.R. King, "Towards a temporal logic based formalism for expressing temporal constraints in multimedia documents," Tech. Report 942, LRI, Paris-Sud university, France, December 1994.
13. T.D.C. Little, Ghafoor A. "Synchronization and Storage Models for Multimedia Objects," Journal on Selected Areas in Communication, Vol. 8, No.3, 1990.
14. F. Maaref, C. Djeraba, and H. Briand, "Synchronization and retrieval multimedia objects model," Proc. National Conference on Compression and Audiovisual Signal Representation, Grenoble, France, February, 1996.
15. M.J. Perez-Luque and T.D.C. Little, "A Temporal Reference Framework for Multimedia Synchronization," In Journal on Selected Areas in Communication, 1995.
16. J.M. Proth and X. XIE, "The Petri nets for the production management systems," Edit. Masson, Paris, 1994.
17. V. Stephan, H. Villaume, and C. Djeraba, "Design and implementation of temporal specification language of scenario generation based on temporal Petri nets," Report of engineering project, December 1995.
18. P.D. Stotts and R. Furuta, "Temporal Hyperprogramming," J. Of Visual Languages and Computing," Vol. 1, 1990 , pp. 237–253.
19. T. Wahl and K. Rothermel, "Representing Time in Multimedia Systems," In Proc. IEEE Intl. Conference on Multimedia Computing and Systems, Boston, USA, May 1994, pp. 538–543.
20. R. Weiss, A. Duda, and D.K. Gifford, "Composition and search with a video Algebra," IEEE Multimedia, 2(1), 1995.

Chabane Djeraba is an assistant professor in the engineering school (IRESTE) at Nantes University, France. He is a member of the computer science research institute of Nantes (IRIN), France, where he is involved in the development of multimedia research for scenario synchronization and content-based multimedia retrieval. He received the B. S. Degree in computer engineering from Algiers computer science national institute (INI, ex. CERI), Algeria, in 1989, the M. S. degree in computer science from Pierre Mendes France university in 1990, and the Ph.D. in computer science from Lyon Claude Bernard University in 1993, France. He has worked on knowl edge and data bases for engineering design, and his current research include multimedia and knowledge discovery in databases.

Karima Hadouda is a Ph.D. candidate in the computer science research institute of Nantes (IRIN), at Nantes University, France. Her research interests include multimedia synchronization in an object oriented database. She received her B. S. and M. S. degree in computer engineering from Oran University, Algeria, in 1984 and 1991. She was research assistant at Oran University until 1991.

Henri Briand is a professor of information system and databases in the Engineering School (IRESTE) at Nantes University. He is in charge of the knowledge and information system research group of the computer science research institute of Nantes (IRIN), France. He developed several fields of research such as distributed object-oriented databases, and knowledge and multimedia databases.

Multimedia Tools and Applications, 4, 115–151 (1997)

The Architecture of the Dalí Main-Memory Storage Manager

PHILIP BOHANNON* bohannon@research.bell-labs.com
DANIEL LIEUWEN lieuwen@research.bell-labs.com
RAJEEV RASTOGI rastogi@research.bell-labs.com
AVI SILBERSCHATZ avi@research.bell-labs.com
Bell Laboratories, 700 Mountain Ave., Murray Hill, NJ 07974

S. SESHADRI seshad@cse.iitb.ernet.edu
S. SUDARSHAN sudarsha@cse.iitb.ernet.edu
Indian Institute of Technology, Bombay, India

Abstract. Performance needs of many database applications dictate that the entire database be stored in main memory. The Dalí system is a main memory storage manager designed to provide the persistence, availability and safety guarantees one typically expects from a disk-resident database, while at the same time providing very high performance by virtue of being tuned to support in-memory data. User processes map the entire database into their address space and access data directly, thus avoiding expensive remote procedure calls and buffer manager interactions typical of accesses in disk-resident commercial systems available today.

Dalí recovers the database to a consistent state in the case of system as well as process failures. It also provides unique concurrency control and memory protection features, as well as ordered and unordered index structures. Both object-oriented and relational database management systems have been implemented on top of Dalí. Dalí provides access to multiple layers of application programming interface, including its low-level recovery, concurrency control and indexing components as well as its high-level relational component. Finally, various features of Dalí can be tailored to the needs of an application to achieve high performance – for example, concurrency control and logging can be turned off if not desired, enabling Dalí to efficiently support applications that require non-persistent memory-resident data to be shared by multiple processes.

Keywords: Main memory database management systems, storage managers

1. Introduction

There are a number of database applications, particularly in the telecommunications industry (and other industries involved in real-time content delivery), where very high performance access to data is required. Such applications typically need high transaction rates, coupled with very low latency for transactions, and impose stringent durability and availability requirements. As an example, consider a real phone-company application where phone call data is recorded, and queries against the data can be issued. The application requires several thousand (albeit small) requests (lookups/updates) to be processed per second, with less than 50 milliseconds latency for lookups, and less than a few minutes of down-time a year. Such applications have been previously implemented as stand-alone programs that run in

* A Ph.D. candidate in the Department of Computer Science at Rutgers University.

main memory and provide their own (usually limited) forms of sharing and persistence mechanisms. It is increasingly being realized that the storage needs of these types of applications would best be met by using an underlying main-memory storage manager that supports an array of functionality such as transaction management, data organization, concurrency control and recovery services. Using the same storage manager across multiple applications can greatly reduce development costs.

The increasing availability of large and relatively cheap memory also suggests that more database applications could reside entirely or almost entirely in main memory. Such applications will experience performance benefits by having data cached in main memory. However, if the storage manager supporting such applications is tailored to main memory, significant additional performance benefits can be achieved, as shown in [27]. Thus, storage managers tailored to main memory would also be ideally suited for such databases.

The Dalí[1] system [22], implemented at Bell Laboratories, is a storage manager for persistent data whose architecture has been optimized for environments in which the database is main-memory resident. While not directly suitable for storing large multimedia objects, Dalí can be used in a number of ways to facilitate delivery of multimedia content. First, it can be used to store *meta-data* such as allocation information about multimedia objects, and has been used in this manner in a prototype of the Fellini continuous media storage server [38]. In such an environment, Dalí may also be used to coordinate shared access to main memory buffers, providing concurrency control and allowing recovery from process failure. Another increasingly significant target application for Dalí is real-time billing and control of multimedia content delivery. In fact, Dalí's original target application, aiding in control and billing for real-time voice data in telephony applications, is just one example of the need for high-speed transactional access to data in multimedia content delivery. We expect a number of new applications in this category to arise from novel content delivery services provided over the World Wide Web.

A number of principles have evolved with Dalí over the past three years and now guide its design and evolution. The first of these principles is *direct access to data.* As described above, we have found that this requirement has already been imposed by the architects of high performance applications. Dalí uses a memory-mapped architecture, where the database is mapped into the virtual address space of the process, allowing the user to acquire pointers directly to information stored in the database. The various interface levels further support the direct access principle by allowing the user access to the data without a copy.[2] A related principle is *no interprocess communication* for basic system services. All concurrency control and logging services are provided via shared memory rather than communication with a server. While Dalí does provide servers to orchestrate system activity, take checkpoints, cope with process failure, etc., a typical user process only communicates with them when connecting to and disconnecting from the database.

The next guiding principle of Dalí is that it enables the creation of *fault-tolerant* applications. The primary expression of this principle is the use of the transactional paradigm, the dominant technology for providing fault-tolerance to critical applications. In fact, Dalí provides an advanced, explicitly multi-level transaction model which has facilitated the production of high-concurrency indexing and storage structures, and the description of this transaction management facility and these storage structures is the primary focus of this paper. The Dalí system also includes other features supporting the principle of fault-tolerance. One is support for recovery from *process failure* in addition to system failure. Another is the use of *codewords* and *memory protection* to help ensure the integrity of data stored in shared memory. Describing these features is a secondary focus of this paper.

Another key requirement for applications which expect to store all their data in main memory is *consistency of response time*. Support for fine-grained concurrency control and minimal interference with the checkpointer due to latching help provide this consistency in Dalí. Other principles that have guided Dalí's implementation have been *a toolkit approach* and support for *multiple interface levels.* The former implies, for example, that logging facilities can be turned off for data which need not be persistent, and locking can be turned off if data is private to a process. The second principle means that low-level components are exposed to the user so that critical system components can be optimized with special implementations. Most applications will prefer the high-level relational and object-oriented interfaces, however.

As a storage manager, Dalí is intended to support a variety of data models – for example, relational and object-oriented models have been implemented in Dalí already. Our intention, like that of the Genesis system [5] and the Exodus Storage Manager [11], is to provide the implementor of a database management system flexible tools for storage management, concurrency control and recovery, without dictating a particular storage model or precluding optimizations. Some of the aspects of Dalí which support this goal are subtle, including a flexible recovery model and storage abstractions which do not build in significant per-item overheads. This last point is particularly important in a main-memory system.

While Dalí can be used in systems where the database is larger than main-memory (as long as the database fits in the virtual address space of the process), the architecture of Dalí, from storage allocation and indexing to its recovery facilities, has been designed to deliver high performance when the database fits into main memory. With minor variations, the version of Dalí described in this paper is currently implemented as a research prototype in Bell Laboratories.[3]

The remainder of the paper is organized as follows. Related work on storage managers and recovery techniques is surveyed in Section 2. In Section 3, we present an overview of the architecture and the storage structures used in Dalí. Details of how Dalí recovers data from system crashes and process failures are given in Sections 4 and 5. Section 6 covers the implementation of latches (semaphores) and locks. Section 7 describes support for collections of data items and indexes, while higher-level relational and object-oriented interfaces are described in Section 8. Finally, concluding remarks are offered in Section 9.

2. Related Work

A storage manager provides the core functionality of a database system, such as concurrency control, recovery mechanisms, storage allocation/free space management, and transaction management. There have been numerous implementations of storage managers for disk resident data. These include the storage managers of Exodus [11], Starburst [18], Object-Store [26], EOS [7], Texas [41], Cricket [40], and QuickStore [45]. After describing how

Dalí relates to other storage managers and main-memory database research in general, we will briefly address related work for the various novel aspects of Dalí's implementation.

With the exception of the Starburst main-memory storage component [27] we are not aware of any storage manager that is tailored for main-memory resident data.[4] The Starburst main-memory storage component is a relational storage manager used as a component of the Starburst database system. Its emphasis is on data allocation and structuring issues; the Starburst main-memory storage component described in [27] uses the recovery manager of Starburst rather than implementing its own recovery manager. In contrast, the recovery mechanisms of Dalí are based on a recovery algorithm tailored to main memory, evolved from those proposed in [23].

Unlike Dalí and the Starburst main-memory storage component, the other (existing or proposed) storage managers of which we are aware are not tailored for memory-resident data. The storage managers for disk-resident data can be divided into two groups. The first group consists of traditional storage managers, such as Exodus and EOS, that provide their own buffer management facilities. The second category consists of storage managers that map the database into virtual memory. Included in this category are the storage manager of ObjectStore, the Texas system, Cricket, and QuickStore.

Storage managers in this second category are more closely related to Dalí, since Dalí also uses a memory-mapped architecture. However, the architecture of existing memory-mapped storage managers, in particular their recovery mechanism, does not take advantage of the database being resident in main memory. For instance, ObjectStore uses page-wise checkpointing, and Texas uses a shadow paging architectures which, while providing support for old versions of data, results in slow commit processing. Also, the storage managers were designed for CAD environments where transactions are long, concurrency control at the level of pages is sufficient, and fast sharing of data is not a primary concern.

Dalí, on the other hand, is designed for high performance applications similar to traditional transaction processing applications but with much lower latency and higher throughput requirements. In a typical Dalí application, transactions are small, multiple processes may access shared data, and high concurrency – especially on index structures – is important. As a result, Dalí supports item level locking. Also, the recovery algorithm used in Dalí is designed to work well with small transactions.

There has been a good deal of prior work in the area of main-memory databases. Much of this work has concentrated on recovery schemes, and will be discussed in the context of other recovery research below. An early paper by DeWitt *et al*, [12], covered a number of topics including query processing, recovery and data organization. A later work by Lehman and Carey on indexing and query evaluation issues, [28], introduced the T-Tree. (A concurrent version of T-Trees is implemented in Dalí.) Garcia-Molina and Salem [15] provide an excellent overview of research on main-memory databases. Lehman *et al.* [27] and Gottemukkala and Lehman [16] discuss the relative costs of operations such as locking and latching in the main-memory storage component of the Starburst extensible database system. They demonstrate that once the I/O bottlenecks of paging data into and out of the database are removed, other factors such as latching and locking dominate the cost of database access, and they provide techniques for reducing such costs. Thus, they provide an excellent motivation for closely examining the system design of a main-memory database and tuning it to remove bottlenecks, and have thereby influenced our work significantly.

Much of the work on main-memory databases has concentrated on recovery [13, 19, 30, 31, 39]. The work by Eich [13] provides a survey, and the performance studies using System M by Salem and Garcia-Molina [39] provide both a good review and performance comparison of many of the schemes suggested by earlier work. Our recovery algorithm is in many ways similar to the "fuzzy" checkpointing schemes of [39], including use of ping-pong checkpointing and dirty page bits. One difference is that updates in Dalí are in-place, requiring that undo information is sometimes necessary. We use the techniques developed for Dalí in [23] to limit this undo logging to during checkpointing so that the majority of undo log information is never written to disk. Our main contribution to this earlier scheme is integration with multi-level recovery, which allows early release of low-level locks for indexing and storage allocation, while retaining the benefits of fuzzy checkpointing for consistency of response times. Multi-level recovery (MLR) schemes have been proposed in the literature [44, 33, 36]. Like these schemes, our scheme repeats history, generates log records during undo processing and logs operation commits when undo operations complete (similar to CLRs described in [36]). Also, as in [33], transaction rollback at crash recovery is performed level-by-level. By integrating MLR with the main-memory recovery techniques described above and in [23], we have produced a significantly optimized multi-level recovery algorithm for main memory database management systems.

As mentioned above, T-trees were proposed by Lehman and Carey in [28]. Our implementation supports concurrent access, scans, and addresses recovery issues. Earlier work on concurrency for binary and AVL trees relates to our work due to the similarity of the structures. The index techniques of [25] do not address all the concurrency control issues needed to implement transaction semantics, while the treatment of [34] requires pre-ordering all accesses to a tree by a given transaction by key value. Neither of [25, 34] address recovery considerations. To our knowledge, no prior work addresses concurrency control and recovery issues for T-trees in particular. Further details of our scheme can be found in [8]. A structure for hashing in main-memory was proposed in [3]. Our hashing structure is much simpler at the cost of more-than-one compare for some searches (no concurrency control scheme was given in [3]). Our concurrency control and recovery mechanisms take advantage of its simplicity; these mechanisms are described in Section 7.2.

The latch recovery techniques are based on work in [9]. A significant body of work on making data structures tolerant to process slow-downs and failures exists under the title of "wait free" data structures (see e.g. [20, 21, 43]). This work is not designed for transaction processing systems, however, and depends on the presence of a compare-and-swap instruction, which is not available in many architectures (such as SPARC). Sullivan and Stonebraker address the problem of protection from erroneous writes in [42], but they assume inexpensive operating system support for protecting and unprotecting data.

3. Architecture

In the Dalí architecture, the database consists of one or more *database files*, along with a special *system database file*. User data itself is stored in database files while all data related

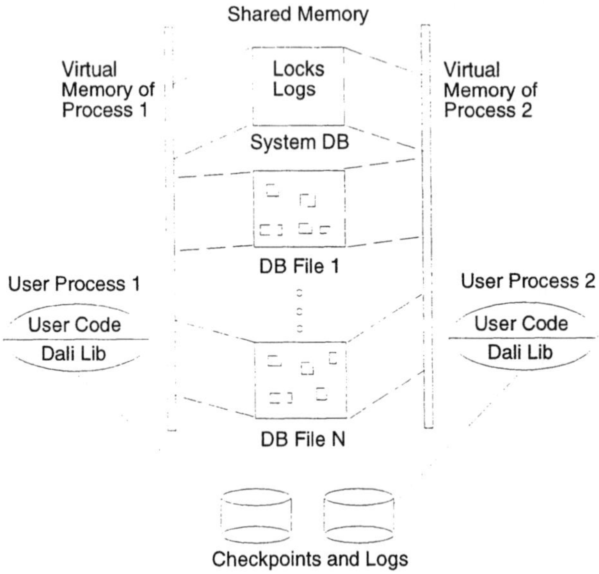

Figure 1. Architecture of the Dalí System

to database support, such as log and lock data, is stored in the system database file. This enables storage allocation routines to be uniformly used for (persistent) user data as well as (non persistent) system data like locks and logs. The system database file also persistently stores information about the database files in the system.

As shown in Figure 1, database files opened by a process are directly mapped into the address space of that process. In Dalí, either memory-mapped files or shared-memory segments can be used to provide this mapping. Different processes may map different sets of database files, and may map the same database file to different locations in their address space.

This feature precludes using virtual memory addresses as physical pointers to data (in database files), but provides two important benefits. First, a database file may be easily resized. Second the total active database space on the system may exceed the addressing space of a single process. This is useful on machines with 32-bit addressing (e.g., the SPARCCenter) in which physical memory can significantly exceed the amount of memory addressable by a single process.

However, in a 64-bit machine, both of these considerations may be significantly mitigated, leading us to consider using physical addressing. If a single database file can be limited to something like 64 Gigabytes, then each process could still map close to a billion database files (which can be expected to far exceed the total database space).

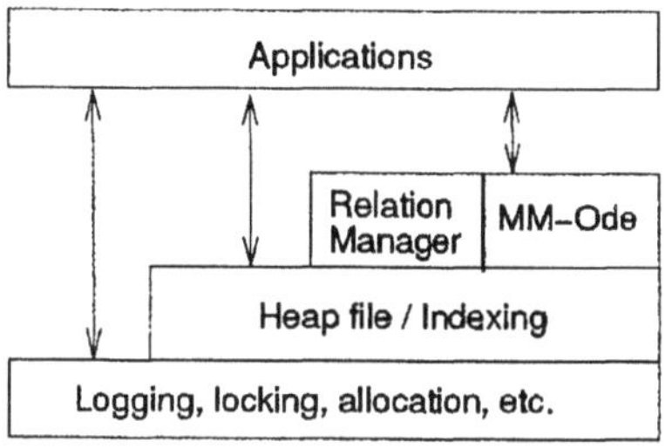

Figure 2. Layers of Abstraction in Dalí

3.1. *Layers of Abstraction*

An important feature of Dalí's architecture is that it is organized in multiple layers of abstraction to support the toolkit approach discussed earlier. Figure 2 illustrates this architecture. At the highest level, users can interact with either Dalí's relational manager or the Main-Memory Ode object database. These two layers are described later in sections 8.1 and 8.2. Below that level is what we call the "heap-file/indexing layer," which provides support for fixed-length and variable-length collections, as well as template-based indexing abstractions. In general, at this level, one does not need to interact with individual locks or latches. Instead, one specifies a policy to the lower level, such as "no locking" or "lock-plus-handle-phantoms".

Services for logging, locking, latching, multi-level recovery and storage allocation are exposed at the lowest level. New indexing methods can be built on this layer, as can special-purpose data structures for either an application or a database management system. Of course, this level has the most complex user-interface, but it has proven itself during the creation of the higher-level interfaces and database systems described above.

3.2. *Pointers and Offsets*

It is crucial for performance that mapping from database pointers to virtual memory addresses be done efficiently. In Dalí, each process maintains a database-offset table, which specifies where in memory each database file is mapped. The table is currently implemented as an array indexed by the (integer) database file identifier.

The primary kind of database pointer in Dalí contains a database file local-identifier and an offset within the database file. Dereferencing a database pointer p simply involves adding the offset contained in p to the virtual memory address at which the database file is mapped, looked up from the offset table. A second form of database pointer is available for cases where the database file is known from context. For example, all pointers out of a certain index might reside in a particular database file. In this case, we may store just the offset within the database file as the pointer. Both offsets and full pointers are implemented as simple C++ template classes which allow them to be used as "smart pointers".

3.3. Storage Allocation

We next describe how storage for data is allocated within a database file. Designing storage allocation structures consists primarily of trading speed for generality and flexibility. Our particular choices are motivated by the following requirements: 1) control data should be stored separately from user data, 2) indirection should not exist at the lowest level, 3) large objects should be stored contiguously, and 4) different recovery characteristics should be available for different areas. We now describe each requirement in more detail.

Control data should be stored separately from user data. Since processes map the entire database file into their address space, stray pointers in applications can easily corrupt the database. Maintaining the integrity of control data (e.g., information about free storage space) is crucial since it's corruption implies the corruption of the entire database file. If control data is stored with the data itself, then the control data would be very susceptible to corruption by simple errors such as improper bounds checking or accessing recently freed memory. However, if control information is stored separately from the data, then stray application pointers are more likely to corrupt other user data rather than control data. Thus, the corruption of the entire database file can be avoided.

Indirection should not exist at the lowest level. Most disk-based storage managers (e.g., Exodus, EOS, System R) have a slotted page architecture in which data is allocated in pages and a slot array at the bottom of the page contains pointers to allocated data. Each data item is then identified by the page containing it and the index of the slot containing a pointer to it. This indirection has the advantage that data items in a page can be moved around in order to reclaim space, and only the pointers in the slots need to be updated. However, the indirection almost certainly adds a level of latching to each data access, as well as adding path length for the dereference itself. Finally, there is an additional storage cost for the extra pointers. In Dalí, since the database is main-memory resident, these costs are proportionally much higher than in a disk resident system. Further, for an object-oriented database, a level of indirection may already exist in the mapping from object identifier to objects which offers many of these advantages, such as the ability to move and resize objects, making the overhead of slotted pages redundant. For these reasons, we did not adopt the slotted page architecture in Dalí. Instead, the storage allocator exposes direct pointers to allocated data providing both time and space efficiency.

Large objects should be stored contiguously. If large objects are stored in main memory, the advantage is obviously speed. Having to reconstruct them from smaller objects will serve to negate that advantage. Thus, Dalí items can be of arbitrary size.

Different recovery characteristics should be available for different regions of the database. Not all data needs to be recovered in case of a system crash. For example, indexes could be recovered by recreating the index (at a substantial cost in recovery time). Similarly, lock and semaphore contents do not need to persist across system crashes – they simply need to be re-initialized at recovery time. We distinguish two levels of non-recovered data: *zeroed memory* and *transient memory*. Zeroed memory remains allocated upon recovery but each byte is set to zero. With transient memory, the data is no longer allocated upon recovery. These characteristics can be applied at the database level, and at the sub-database level as described in the next section.

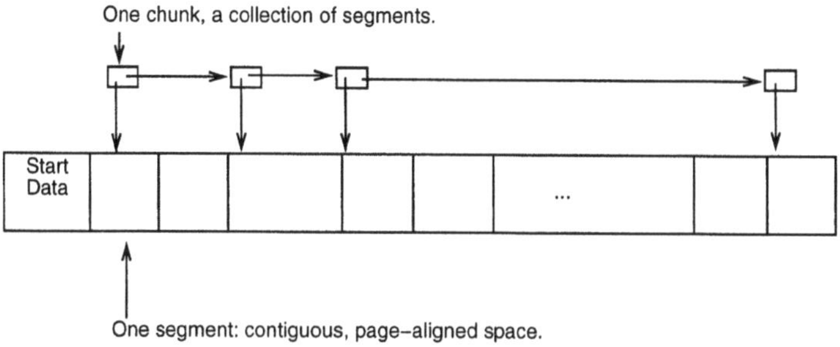

Figure 3. Segments and Chunks

3.3.1. Segments and Chunks

We now describe the storage allocation mechanism in Dalí, and show how it meets the requirements described above. Each database file in Dalí is comprised of *segments*, which are contiguous page-aligned units of allocation, similar to clusters in a file system. As illustrated in Figure 3, a *chunk* is a collection of segments. Recovery characteristics (transient memory, zeroed memory, or persistent memory) are specified on a per-chunk basis at the time of chunk creation. Users allocate within a chunk, and do not specify a particular segment. Since segments can be arbitrarily large (within the size of the database), arbitrarily large objects can be stored contiguously. Upon allocation within a chunk, the system returns a standard Dalí pointer to the space, which specifies the offset within the file. Thus, indirection is not imposed at the storage manager level. The elements shown linking together segments in a chunk are themselves stored in a special chunk used for control information.

Within a chunk, different allocators are available which trade off speed, safety and size. In all allocators, no record of allocated space is retained, and the user must remember the size of the allocated data. This is required to avoid excessive overhead for small items. A layer above the allocator can be implemented to store this data above the allocated space, if required. The currently defined and implemented allocators in Dalí are

- The *power-of-two allocator* allocates storage in buckets of size $2^i * m$ where m is some minimum item size.

- The *inline power-of-two allocator* is the same except that the free space list uses the first few bytes of each free block to implement the list.

- The *coalescing allocator* merges adjacent free space and uses a *free tree*, described below.

In both power-of-two allocators, space requests are rounded up to a bucket size. Free-space lists are maintained per-bucket, where a bucket represents an allocation size, with a maximum item size of $2^{31} * m$. Free-space lists are stored in a *separate* chunk, making it much harder for simple programming errors to corrupt the system-wide free space tables. Requested (freed) space that is rounded up to size $2^i * m$ is allocated (freed) from (to) the ith bucket. The inline allocator is faster and more space efficient, but susceptible to corruption from simple off-by-one programming errors. This allocator is mostly used for system-maintained data (such as the free space lists for the power-of-two allocator). Since the power-of-two allocators do not coalesce adjacent free space, they are subject to fragmentation and are thus primarily used for fixed size data.

The coalescing allocator provided by Dalí is implemented using a *free tree*. Our implementation of this structure is based on the T-tree described in Section 7.3. It consists of a T-tree of free space which uses the starting address of free blocks as the key. Thus, any two free blocks which are candidates to be merged will be adjacent in the tree. Each node is annotated with the largest free block in the subtree rooted at that node. This information is used during allocation to traverse the free tree – at each node the subtree chosen is one which contains a free block larger than the requested size. Traversal halts once a sufficiently large free block is found. Each time space is freed, it is inserted into the free tree and an attempt is made to merge it with its in-order successor and predecessor in the tree. In the case that allocation or freeing of space causes the sizes of free blocks in the free tree to change, this information is propagated upwards to all the ancestors of the node in the free tree, if necessary. This structure provides logarithmic time for both allocation and freeing, while keeping all adjacent free space coalesced and providing exact allocation.

In the allocation schemes described above, contiguous unallocated space at the end of the last segment for the chunk is not contained in the free lists and the free tree. Thus, if no free blocks are found in the free lists or the free tree, space is allocated from the end of the last segment in the chunk if possible. If sufficient space is not available at the end of the last segment, then a new segment is allocated for the chunk from the database file and space is allocated from it (the new segment is also appended to the list of segments for the chunk, and the insufficient free space in the former last segment is added to free space list).

3.3.2. The Page Table and Segment Headers

Database systems which use physical addressing may need to associate some information about the segment or the chunk with a physical database pointer. For this reason, we have implemented *segment headers* in Dalí, and use a *page table* to map pages to segment headers. The page table is pre-allocated based on the maximum number of pages in the database (and reallocated if the database is resized). Segment headers are allocated when a new segment is added to a chunk. Furthermore, each page table entry corresponding to a page in the newly-allocated segment is updated to point to the segment header for the segment. The segment header, in addition to containing the start address for the segment and the chunk containing the segment, can also contain additional information about data in the segment to support higher-level abstractions (e.g., lock and type information). This last facility is used by the heap file described in Section 7.1.

4. Transaction Management in Dalí

In this section we describe how transaction atomicity, isolation and durability are achieved in Dalí. Transaction management in Dalí is based on principles of multi-level recovery [44, 36, 33]. To our knowledge, Dalí is the only implementation of multi-level recovery for main-memory, and one of the few implementations of explicit multi-level recovery reported to date (Weikum [44] reports use of explicit MLR in a prototype database management system).

We begin with a review of multi-level recovery concepts, followed by a description of the structures used in Dalí for transactions, logging and other recovery support mechanisms. Our implementation extends the scheme presented in [23] with multiple levels of abstraction, and a fuzzy checkpointing scheme that only writes dirty pages. Low-level details of our scheme are described in [10].

In our scheme, data is logically organized into *regions*. A region can be a tuple, an object, or an arbitrary data structure like a list or a tree. Each region has a single associated lock with exclusive (X) and shared (S) modes, referred to as the *region lock*, that guards accesses and updates to the region.

4.1. Multi-Level Recovery

Multi-level recovery provides recovery support for enhanced concurrency based on the semantics of operations. Specifically, it permits the use of weaker *operation* locks in place of stronger shared/exclusive region locks.

A common example is index management, where holding physical locks until transaction commit leads to unacceptably low levels of concurrency. If undo logging has been done physically (e.g. recording exactly which bytes were modified to insert a key into the index) then the transaction management system must ensure that these physical-undo descriptions are valid until transaction commit. Since the descriptions refer to specific updates at specific positions, this typically implies that the region locks on the updated index nodes are retained to ensure correct *recovery*, even though they are no longer needed for correct concurrent access to the index.

The multi-level recovery approach is to replace these low-level physical-undo log records with higher-level logical-undo log records containing undo descriptions at the operation level. Thus, for an insert operation, physical-undo records would be replaced by a logical-undo record indicating that the inserted key must be deleted. Once this replacement is made, the region locks may be released, and only (less restrictive) operation locks are retained. For example, region locks on the particular nodes involved in an insert can be released, while an operation lock on the newly inserted key that prevents the key from being accessed or deleted is retained.

We illustrate multi-level recovery under this model. Consider a unique hash index that stores a <key value, pointer to record> pair for every record in a database. Let the hash index support operations insert, delete and find with the obvious meanings.

Note that each operation takes a key value as a parameter; it is on this key value that the operation gets an operation lock when it begins. Operation locks here are of three kinds:

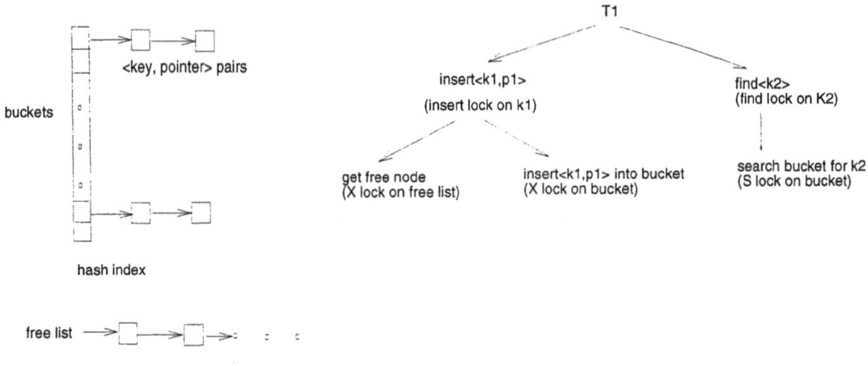

Figure 4. Overview of Multi-level Recovery

insert, delete and find locks. Operation locks on different key values do not conflict with each other. Furthermore, insert and delete locks conflict with every other operation lock (find/insert/delete) on the same key value; however, find locks on the same key value do not conflict with each other.

In order to see how operation locking can help enhance concurrency, consider an implementation of the hash index with buckets, (see Figure 4), where each bucket points to a linked list of nodes, each node containing a single <key value, record pointer> pair. In this implementation, it was decided that each bucket including the linked list constitute a region, and thus one region lock is associated with one bucket. In addition, there is also a free list of nodes from which nodes are obtained when inserting into the hash index. The free list is a separate region with its own lock.

A find operation obtains a find operation lock on the key value, and then an S region lock on the bucket containing the key value and releases the lock on the bucket once the node in the bucket chain containing the key value has been found. However, the find lock on the key-value is held for the duration of the transaction.

An insert operation first obtains an insert operation lock on the key value, and then obtains a region lock on the free list in X mode, and deletes a node from the free list. It then determines the bucket into which the key value is to be inserted and obtains an X region lock on the bucket. It then copies the <key value, pointer> pair into the free node and links the node into the bucket chain. Obtaining the free node and linking it into the bucket chain result in several updates, which are all *physically* logged. Once the node has been added to the chain, the insert operation is complete. At this point, the physical-undo log records are deleted and replaced by a logical-undo log record, which if executed, would call the delete operation on the new <key value, record pointer> pair. Also, the X region locks on the free list and the bucket are no longer required, and are released. Only the insert operation lock is held till end of transaction.

Note that if the physical-undo log records were not replaced by the logical-undo log record, it would not have been possible to release locks on the free list and the bucket. Once the region locks are released, other operations can update the same regions (bucket and free list),

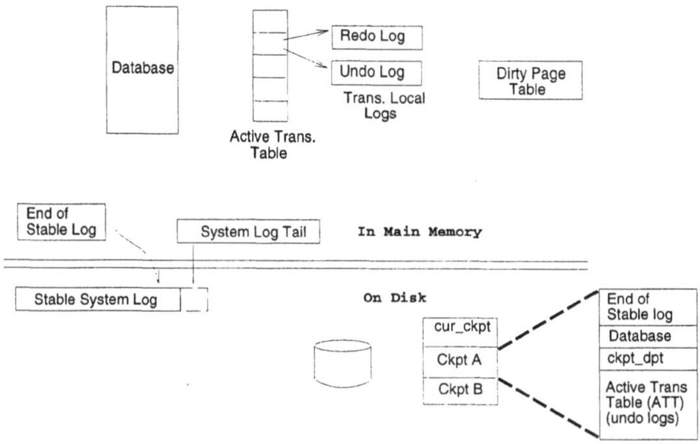

Figure 5. Overview of Recovery Structures

and attempting to roll back the first operation using physical-undo records would damage the effects of the later actions. Once the region locks are released, only a compensating undo operation can be used to undo the operation. The replacement of lower-level undo operations by higher-level undo operations is, in a nutshell, the idea underlying multi-level recovery. Without multi-level recovery, other allocation operations on the storage allocator would have been blocked until the end of the transaction – resulting in a lower degree of concurrency. Multi-level recovery is supported in, for example, ARIES [36].

4.2. System Overview

Figure 5 gives an overview of the structures used for recovery. The database[5] is mapped into the address space of each process as described in Section 3. Two checkpoint images of the database, Ckpt_A and Ckpt_B, reside on disk. Also stored on disk are 1) cur_ckpt, an "anchor" pointing to the most recent valid checkpoint image for the database, and 2) a single system log containing redo information, with its tail in memory. The variable end_of_stable_log stores a pointer into the system log such that all records prior to the pointer are known to have been flushed to the stable system log.

There is a single *active transaction table* (ATT), stored in the system database, that stores separate redo and undo logs for each active transaction. A dirty page table, dpt, is maintained for the database (also in the system database) which records the pages that have been updated since the last checkpoint. The ATT (with undo logs) and the dirty page table are also stored with each checkpoint. The dirty page table in a checkpoint is referred to as ckpt_dpt.

4.3. *Transactions and Operations*

Transactions, in our model, consist of a sequence of operations. Similar to [33], we assume that each operation has a level L_i associated with it. An operation at level L_i can consist of a sequence of operations at level L_{i-1}. Transactions, assumed to be at level L_n, call operations at level L_{n-1}. Physical updates to regions are level L_0 operations. For transactions, we distinguish between *pre-commit*, when the commit record enters the system log in memory establishing a point in the serialization order, and *commit* when the commit record hits the stable log. We use the same terminology for operations, where only the pre-commit point is meaningful, though this is sometimes referred to as "operation commit" in the paper.

Each transaction obtains an *operation* lock before an operation executes (the lock is granted to the operation if it commutes with other operation locks held by active transactions), and L_0 operations must obtain region locks. The locks on the region are released once the L_1 operation pre-commits; however, an operation lock at level L_i is held until the transaction or the containing operation (at level L_{i+1}) pre-commits. Thus, all the locks acquired by a transaction are released once it pre-commits. The notion of pre-commit for transactions and a locking optimization related to the one implemented in Dalí is described in [12].

4.4. *Logging Model*

The recovery algorithm maintains separate undo and redo logs in memory for each transaction. These are stored as linked lists off the entry for the transaction in the ATT. Each update (to a part of a region) generates physical-undo and redo log records that are appended to the transaction's undo and redo logs respectively. When a transaction/operation pre-commits, all the redo log records for the transaction in its redo log are appended to the system log, and the logical-undo description for the operation is included in the operation commit log record in the system log. Thus, with the exception of logical-undo descriptors, only redo records are written to the system log during normal processing.

Also, when an operation pre-commits, the undo log records for its sub-operations/updates are deleted (from the transaction's undo log) and a logical-undo log record containing the undo description for the operation is appended to the transaction's undo log. In-memory undo logs of transactions that have pre-committed are deleted since they are not required again. Locks acquired by an operation/transaction are released once they pre-commit.

The system log is flushed to disk when a transaction decides to commit. Pages updated by a redo log record written to disk are marked dirty in the dirty page table, dpt, by the flushing procedure. In our recovery scheme, update actions do not obtain latches on pages – instead region locks ensure that updates do not interfere with each other.[6] In addition, actions that are normally taken on page latching, such as setting of dirty bits for the page, are now performed based on log records written to the redo log. For example, the flusher uses physical log records to set per-page dirty bits, avoiding contention on the dirty page table. The redo log is used as a single unifying resource to coordinate the applications interaction with the recovery system, and this approach has proven very useful.

4.5. Ping-pong Checkpointing

Consistent with the terminology in main-memory databases, we use the term *checkpoint* to mean a copy of main-memory, stored on disk, and *checkpointing* refers to the action of creating a checkpoint. This terminology differs slightly from the terminology used, for example, in ARIES [36].

Traditional recovery schemes implement write-ahead logging (WAL), whereby all undo logs for updates on a page are flushed to disk before the page is flushed to disk. To guarantee the WAL property, a latch on the page (or possibly on the system log) is held while copying the page to disk. In our recovery scheme, we eliminate latches on pages during updates, since latching can significantly increase access costs in main memory and interferes with normal processing, as well as increasing programming complexity. However, as a result, it is not possible to enforce the WAL policy, since pages may be updated even as they are being written out.

For correctness, in the absence of write-ahead logging, two copies of the database image are stored on disk, and alternate checkpoints write dirty pages to alternate copies. This strategy is called *ping-pong* checkpointing (see, e.g., [?]). The ping-pong checkpointing strategy permits a checkpoint that is being created to be temporarily inconsistent; i.e., updates may have been written out without corresponding undo records having been written. However, after writing out dirty pages, sufficient redo and undo log information is written out to bring the checkpoint to a consistent state. Even if a failure occurs while creating one checkpoint, the other checkpoint is still consistent and can be used for recovery.

Keeping two copies of a main-memory database on disk for ping-pong checkpointing does not have a very high space penalty, since disk space is much cheaper than main-memory. As we shall see later, there is an I/O penalty in that dirty pages have to be written out to both checkpoints even if there was only one update on the page. However, this penalty is small for hot pages, and the benefits outweigh the I/O cost for typical main-memory database applications.

Before writing any dirty data to disk, the checkpoint notes the current end of the stable log in the variable end_of_stable_log, which will be stored with the checkpoint. This is the start point for scanning the system log when recovering from a crash using this checkpoint. Next, the contents of the (in-memory) ckpt_dpt are set to those of the dpt and the dpt is zeroed (noting of end_of_stable_log and zeroing of dpt are done atomically with respect to flushing). The pages written out are the pages that were either dirty in the ckpt_dpt of the last completed checkpoint, or dirty in the current (in-memory) ckpt_dpt, or in both. In other words, all pages that were modified since the current checkpoint image was last written, namely, pages that were dirtied since the last-but-one checkpoint, are written out. This is necessary to ensure that updates described by log records preceding the current checkpoint's end_of_stable_log have made it in the database image in the current checkpoint.

Checkpoints write out dirty pages without obtaining any latches and thus without interfering with normal operations. This *fuzzy* checkpointing is possible since physical-redo log records are generated by all updates; these are used during restart recovery and their effects are idempotent. For any uncommitted update whose effects have made it to the checkpoint image, undo log records would be written out to disk after the database image has been written. This is performed by checkpointing the ATT after checkpointing the data; the checkpoint of the ATT writes out undo log records, as well as some other status information.

At the end of checkpointing, a log flush must be done before declaring the checkpoint completed (and consistent) by toggling cur_ckpt to point to the new checkpoint, for the following reason. Undo logs are deleted on transaction/operation pre-commit, which may happen before the checkpoint of the ATT. If the checkpoint completes, and the system then fails before a log flush, then the checkpoint may contain uncommitted updates for which there is no undo information. The log flush ensures that the transaction/operation has committed, and so the updates will not have to be undone (except perhaps by a compensating operation, for which undo information will be present in the log).

4.6. *Abort Processing*

When a transaction aborts, that is, does not successfully complete execution, updates/operations described by log records in the transaction's undo log are undone by traversing the undo log sequentially from the end. Transaction abort is carried out by executing, in reverse order, every undo record just as if the execution were part of the transaction.

Following the philosophy of *repeating history* [36], new physical-redo log records are created for each physical-undo record encountered during the abort. Similarly, for each logical-undo record encountered, a new "compensation" or "proxy" operation is executed based on the undo description. Log records for updates performed by the operation are generated as during normal processing. Furthermore, when the proxy operation commits, all its undo log records are deleted along with the logical-undo record for the operation that was undone. The commit record for the proxy operation serves a purpose similar to that served by *compensation log records* (CLRs) in ARIES – during restart recovery, when it is encountered, the logical-undo log record for the operation that was undone is deleted from the transaction's undo log, thus preventing it from being undone again.

4.7. *Recovery*

As part of the checkpoint operation, the end-of-the-system-log on disk is noted before the database image is checkpointed, and becomes the "begin-recovery-point" for this checkpoint once the checkpoint has completed. All updates described by log records preceding this point are guaranteed to be reflected in the checkpointed database image. Thus, restart recovery, after initializing the ATT and transaction undo logs with the copy of the ATT and undo logs stored in the most recent checkpoint, loads the database image and sets dpt to zero. It then applies all redo log records following the begin-recovery-point for the last completed checkpoint of the database (appropriate pages in dpt are set to dirty for each log record). During the application of redo log records, necessary actions are taken to keep the checkpointed image of the ATT consistent with the log applied so far. These actions mirror the actions taken during normal processing. For example, when an operation commit log record is encountered, lower-level log records in the transaction's undo log for the operation are replaced by a higher-level undo description.

Once all the redo log records have been applied, the active transactions are rolled back. To do this, all completed operations that have been invoked directly by the transaction, or have been directly invoked by an incomplete operation have to be rolled back. However, the order in which operations of different transactions are rolled back is very important, so that an undo at level L_i sees data structures that are consistent [33]. First, all operations (across all transactions) at L_0 that must be rolled back are rolled back, followed by all operations at level L_1, then L_2 and so on.

Note that for certain uncommitted updates present in the redo log, undo log records may not have been recorded during the checkpoint – this could happen for instance when an operation executes and commits after the checkpoint, and the containing transaction has not committed. However, this is not a problem since the undo description for the operation would have been found in operation commit log records during the forward pass over the system log earlier during recovery. Any redo log records for updates performed by an operation whose commit log record is not found in the system log are ignored (since these must be due to a crash during flush and are at the tail of the system log).

4.8. Post-commit Operations

Some types of operations that a transaction may need to execute cannot be rolled back. For example, consider the deletion of a record from the database when physical pointers are employed. If the space for the record were de-allocated as part of the delete, then problems may be encountered during rollback if the transaction were to abort. The reason for this is that, for high concurrency, we need to permit storage allocation and de-allocation to continue once the space for the record was de-allocated but before the transaction (or operation) that de-allocated the space committed. As a result, the space may potentially be allocated by another transaction, making it impossible for the transaction that freed it to re-obtain it in case it were to abort. Thus, new storage space would need to be allocated for the record and old references/pointers to the record (e.g., in the index) may no longer be valid.

The above problem can be avoided by using the notion of *post commit operations*, that is, operations that are guaranteed to be carried out after the commit of a transaction or operation, even in the face of system/process failure. (Recoverable queues are used for the same purpose in other systems [6].) Transaction operations that cannot be undone can be performed as post-commit operations, preserving the all-or-nothing property of the transaction. Thus, by executing the de-allocation of storage space for the record as a post-commit operation, we can permit high concurrency on the storage allocator (no transaction duration locks on the allocator are required), and at the same time, ensure that space gets de-allocated if the transaction commits, whether or not the system fails after the commit. This facility is also valuable for implementing externally visible writes, such as sending a message on commit of a transaction, which are especially important in work-flow situations. Similarly, the notion of post-commit operations can be extended to operations by permitting an operation at level L_i to require post-commit operations at level L_{i-1} to be executed once it pre-commits.

A separate post-commit log is maintained for each transaction – every log record contains the description of a post-commit operation to be executed. These are appended to the system log immediately before the commit record for a transaction (when it pre-commits) or immediately before the operation commit record when the operation pre-commits. Once transaction commit/operation pre-commit completes, the post-commit operations are executed. Furthermore, the checkpoint of the ATT writes out post-commit log records along with undo log records for the transaction. Thus, for every committed transaction, post-commit log records for the transaction are contained on disk, in the log, and possibly also in the checkpointed ATT (in cases where post-commit log records in the log precede the begin-recovery point). As a result, during restart recovery, the post-commit operations can be determined and executed for transactions that were in the process of executing post-commit operations when the system crashed.

5. Fault Tolerance

In this section, we present features for fault tolerant programming in Dalí, other than those provided directly by transaction management. These techniques help cope with process failure scenarios. The first technique returns the system to a fully available state if a process dies with transactions in progress. The second and third techniques help detect and recover from user programs with "stray pointers" which might corrupt persistent data stored in shared memory.

5.1. Process Death

In this section, we discuss how Dalí handles "untimely" process death. This may be caused by the process violating hardware protection such as attempting to access invalid memory, or by a process being killed by an operator. In either case, we assume that the process did not corrupt any system control structures. Recovering from process death primarily consists of returning any shared data partially updated by the process to a consistent state. Since no volatile memory has been lost, this is in some ways easier than crash recovery. However, during crash recovery, one can assume that internal system structures (such as the transaction table and lock tables) are in a consistent state, as they are recreated on recovery. It is the lack of this low-level consistency which complicates process recovery.

Obviously, the main approach to handling a dead process is to abort any uncommitted transactions owned by that process. Also, in our system, for committed transactions and pre-committed operations, post-commit actions must also be executed on behalf of the process. However, this cannot be begun immediately upon determining that a process died. That process may hold latches on low-level system structures, such as the system log. Any attempt to abort a transaction would attempt to get that latch, causing the process attempting to clean up the resource to wait on the (dead) process it is trying to clean up. Thus, process recovery must be done carefully.

A Dalí system process known as the *cleanup server* is primarily responsible for handling the cleanup of dead processes. We now describe the actions taken by this server.

5.1.1. *Detecting Process Death*

The first step in cleanup of crashed processes is to detect that a process crashed. When a process connects to the Dalí system, information about the process such as its operating system process identifier are noted in an Active Process Table in the system database. Dalí server processes also register themselves in the same table. When a process terminates its connection via DaliSys::close(), it is deregistered from the table. The cleanup process periodically goes through the table and checks (via the operating system) if each registered process is still alive.

If a registered process is found not to exist, cleanup actions have to be taken.

5.1.2. *Low Level Cleanup*

Once a dead process has been found, the cleanup process determines what low-level latches, if any, were held by the crashed process. Whenever a process acquires a latch, an entry is made in the Active Process Table.[7] This table is consulted by the cleanup process to determine if the process was holding a latch. The detection is complicated significantly by the fact that in many machine architectures it is not possible to atomically acquire a spin-lock and register ownership. A technique for getting around the problem is presented in Section 6.1.

If any system latches are held by the process, then a cleanup function associated with the latch is called. This is an example of a "functional recovery procedure" and may require that a few words of undo information be stored in the system structure. A special return code is reserved to indicate that the structure could not be repaired by this function. In this case, the system must simulate a full crash, causing a recovery which does not depend on the corrupted structure (or any other transient system data).

However, if the dead process did not hold any such latches, or if the latches it held were successfully cleaned up, then the cleanup server may proceed to the next phase which involves cleaning up transactions owned by the dead process.

5.1.3. *Cleaning Up Transactions*

Once low-level structures have been restored to a consistent state, the cleanup server spawns a new process, called a *cleanup agent*, to take care of cleaning up any transactions still running on behalf of this process. This amounts to scanning the transaction table, and aborting any in-progress transactions owned by the dead process, or executing any post-commit actions for a committed transaction which had not been executed.

Two subtle points arise here. First, the in-progress transaction may have already started an abort. Similarly, the dead process may have been executing its post-commit actions.

Thus, the transaction must indicate during these activities (and in fact during all activities) whether the transaction table entry for that transaction is in a consistent state. If not, then that is handled as if the process held a low-level latch, which is described above.

The subtle point concerns the case that multiple processes have died, or the case that a new process dies while the old one was being cleaned up. In these cases, the cleanup server must spawn multiple cleanup agents concurrently. This is required since a transaction for one dead process may have to wait for a resource held by another dead process in order for it to complete its abort. (Note that these locks must be at lower levels of abstraction than the transaction level, as a transaction level lock would have been held by the transaction until commit and thus not need to be reacquired.) If the dead process were threaded, the cleanup agent must include a separate thread for each active transaction for the same reason.

5.2. *Protection from Application Errors*

The direct access principle of Dalí implies that at least some user application code will be linked directly with Dalí libraries and access the data stored in the database through shared memory. With this comes the inevitable chance that an application error will lead to writes which can cause persistent data to become corrupted. Dalí provides two mechanisms for minimizing the probability that such errors will lead to corrupting persistent data. The first mechanism is *memory protection* and the second is *codewords.*

Both mechanisms are designed only to prevent updates which are not correctly logged from becoming reflected in the permanent database. This would occur if a database pointer used for direct memory access were used later for an update as if it were a normal pointer. Similarly, such a problem might occur due to a random garbage value in a pointer. This second case becomes much more probable as database sizes approach virtual memory address range sizes. This is very conceivable in modern 32-bit systems, where it is very reasonable to find multiple gigabytes of RAM.

These mechanisms do not protect from erroneous updates which follow the proper database conventions. Nor are they capable of protecting from *all* erroneous updates which do not use database conventions, and such limits are described for each scheme. However, these schemes vastly reduce the probability that a programming error can corrupt the persistent database. The codeword scheme also protects against bit errors in memory, which are a significant worry with gigabytes of RAM.

The schemes are independent, and can be used in conjunction.

5.2.1. *Memory Protection*

Applications wishing to prevent corruption due to stray pointers can map a database file in a special protected mode. For such database files, Dalí uses the mprotect system call to disable updates to the file by the process. Before a page is updated, when an undo log record for the update is generated, munprotect is called on the page. At the end of the transaction, all the unprotected pages are re-protected. Thus, an erroneous update would attempt to update a protected page, thus resulting in a protection violation. The advantage of this scheme is that erroneous writes are detected immediately, and can be traced to their source using a debugger. The disadvantage is that the system calls are a significant performance hit. As a result, this scheme is more beneficial when debugging applications, and for read-only databases or databases with low update rates. Note also that since unprotected pages stay unprotected until the end of transaction, erroneous writes in a transaction following a correct write to the same page will not be detected with this scheme.

5.2.2. Codewords

The codeword strategy of error detection is to associate a logical parity word with each page of data. Whenever data is updated using valid Dalí system calls, the codeword is updated accordingly. An erroneous write will update only the physical data and not the codeword. We then use the strategy of protecting the checkpoint image on disk. Before writing a page to a checkpoint, its contents are verified against the codeword for that page. Should a mismatch be found, a simulated system crash is caused, and the database is recovered from the last checkpoint.

Our current implementation of codewords, based on page-level latching, is as follows. Each page has an associated latch and codeword. While updating a page, the latch for the page is held in shared mode by the updater. At the end, the change to the codeword for the page is computed from the current contents of the updated region, and the contents of the region before the update (this is determined from the physical undo log record for the update). A short term exclusive latch on the codeword table is then obtained to actually apply the computed change to the codeword value for the page. The latch ensures that concurrent updaters to different regions on a page do not install an incorrect value for the codeword. The checkpointer, on attempting to checkpoint a page, obtains an exclusive latch on the page long enough to copy it and the codeword associated with it to a separate area. The codeword for the copy is then computed and compared with the value from the table.

This implementation is the only use of page-level latching in Dalí. Note that we are currently designing a new scheme which uses the global redo log to avoid this page latching. We expect this will reduce blocking as well as the performance cost associated with the codeword scheme.

The advantages of codewords over memory protection are that lower overhead is incurred during normal updates, and it is less likely that an application error will escape detection. For example, an erroneous write to a page which has just been updated *will* be caught. The disadvantage is that erroneous writes are not detected immediately, making debugging based on this information difficult. (We do allow user-driven codeword audits to make debugging with codewords possible.)

6. Concurrency Control

In this section we describe the concurrency control facilities available in Dalí. These facilities include latches (low-level locks for mutual exclusion) and queueing locks. Our latch implementation is novel in its contribution to recovery from process failure, and our lock implementation makes the task of adding new locking modes trivially easy.

6.1. Latch Implementation

Latches in Dalí are implemented using the atomic instructions supplied by the underlying architecture. The decision to implement latches in Dalí was made since operating system semaphores are too expensive due to the overhead of making system calls. However, to support the process failure scenarios described above, there are certain issues that must be dealt with. First, regardless of the type of atomic instruction available, the fact that the process holds or may hold a latch must be observable by the cleanup server (see Section 5.1) so that it can determine that a dead process held a system resource. This is implemented by maintaining an array of pointers to held (or possibly held) latches from a process's entry in the Active Process List.

However, if the target architecture provides only test-and-set or register-memory-swap as atomic instructions (as opposed to compare-and-swap or load-linked/store-conditional), then extra care must be taken to determine if the process did in fact own the latch. In this section, we provide an overview of the technique used to handle this in Dalí, which is based on [9].

To allow the cleanup server to determine ownership of the latch, a process having acquired a latch must also register itself as the owner, for example by writing its process identifier to a known location. Unfortunately, the act of acquiring the latch using the basic hardware instruction test-and-set (or register-memory-swap) cannot be used to also atomically register ownership. At best, the atomic instruction can be followed by a conditional branch testing for a successful acquisition, which can be followed by an instruction writing the process id of the new owner. If the process that is trying to acquire a latch is interrupted between the test-and-set and the write, the ownership of a latch is left in doubt until the process gets to execute the write. If the process fails in this interval, the ownership of the latch will never become clear. Worse still, it is impossible to distinguish between a process that has failed at this step and a process that has not failed, but has not yet carried out the write, either because it is servicing an interrupt, or because it has not been allocated CPU cycles. A symmetric problem can also arise when releasing the semaphore, since the de-registration and release may have to be accomplished using separate instructions (depending on the exact atomic instruction used).

Although acquisition and registration are separate operations and cannot be executed atomically, we now present an overview of the technique used in Dalí to examine the status of *other* processes that are attempting acquisition of a latch and thereby determine ownership.

We now present the intuition behind our approach. Details of our algorithms are presented in [9].

Consider an atomic test-and-set based implementation of a latch. The first and most obvious step in tracking ownership of such a latch is to require that a successful attempt to acquire the test-and-set latch be immediately followed by a write which stores the new owner's identifier (process or thread identifier, which we abbreviate to *process id*) in an

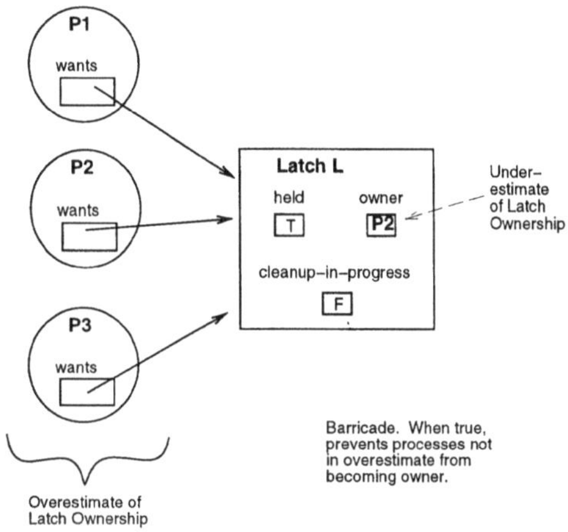

Figure 6. Overview of Latch Control Information

owner field associated with the latch. Clearly, if these two steps were atomic, we could always find out which process currently owns the latch. (Note that if a compare-and-swap instruction is available, the two steps *can* be made atomic.)

Unfortunately, detection of ownership is complicated by the fact that processes may get interrupted, and may even be killed, in between acquisition and registration, and thus a latch may be in a state where it has been acquired by some process, but we do not know which one.

As a first step toward solving these problems, we require that all processes that are trying to acquire a latch keep a pointer to that latch in a per-process shared location. We call this location the process's wants field. The collection of all processes' wants fields provides us with an overestimate of the set of possible owners of the latch (there are zero or one owners, but an arbitrary number of "interested" parties). This helps establish a set of all processes that might hold the latch.

As described in Section 5.1, a *cleanup server* handles recovery from process failure. The first step it takes on detecting the death of a process is to determine if that process held the latch, if any, pointed to by its wants field. If that process is also the owner of the latch, then the work is done. If it is not, the ownership is ambiguous, and the cleanup server must examine the wants field for all processes,

The set of processes that want the latch may, however, change even as the cleanup server attempts to determine which processes have set their "wants" field. To solve this problem, we introduce a flag associated with the latch called cleanup-in-progress, and forbid processes to attempt to get the latch if this flag is set. This flag provides a barrier which, when "raised" (set to True), prevents any new processes from becoming owners of the latch. The cleanup-in-progress flag for a particular latch is set by the cleanup process while it attempts to resolve the ownership of that latch. Without this "barricade," the (remote) possibility exists that one or more processes can repeatedly acquire and release the latch, always leaving the latch acquired but unregistered while its status is tested by the cleanup process. We cannot distinguish between this case and the death of a single process in an indeterminate state. The data structures used by our system latches are summarized in Figure 6. The method described in the rest of this section avoids these problems, and guarantees resolution of the latch if all live processes receive CPU time. (Actually, extensions to handle starved processes have also been developed and are used in Dalí.)

The acquisition protocol of a simple spin-lock implementation is modified so that the process starts by setting its wants field to point to the latch. It then checks cleanup-in-progress for the latch. If a cleanup is found to be in progress, wants is set back to null, and the process waits for the cleanup to end before retrying. Otherwise, it attempts to acquire the lock with a test-and-set instruction.

Given these additional tools, how does the cleanup server determine whether a dead process holds a latch? It starts by setting the cleanup-in-progress flag to True, then gathering a list of potential owners from the wants variables for each process. Now it becomes reasonable to wait until the situation resolves itself, as we must only wait for a finite number of processes to give up their interest in, or register their ownership of, the latch. We do this by removing a process from the list of potential owners when it dies or sets its wants variable to point to null or another lock. In all cases, a process must only advance by a few instructions to either register ownership, or notice that the cleanup-in-progress flag is set, and relinquish its interest in the latch. Should our list of potential owners become empty, we can conclude that the owner is dead. Further, if we reach this conclusion, and yet there is no *registered* owner for the latch, we may conclude that the owner had just acquired it or was about to release it, and thus the system structure guarded by the latch could not be in an inconsistent state. However, if during this cleanup process we find that a dead process is the registered owner, then the cleanup function associated with this latch must be called, as described in Section 5.1.

6.2. Locking System

Having discussed latching, we turn to locking, usually used as the mechanism for concurrency control at the level of a transaction. Locks are normally used to guard accesses to persistent data, and can support modes richer than shared and exclusive. At the lowest level, lock requests in Dalí are made on a lock header structure which simply stores a pointer to a list of locks that have been requested (but not yet been released) by transactions. A lock request that does not conflict with outstanding locks on the lock header is granted. Lock requests that conflict are handled by adding the requested lock to the list of locks for the lock header, and are granted when the conflicting locks are released. If a lock request cannot be granted within a certain interval (specified at system startup time), then the request simply times out. Users can thus pre-allocate lock headers and associate each lock header with a data structure to be locked.

Lock requests in Dalí can also be made on 64-bit lock names which are mapped internally by the Dalí system to lock headers via a hash table. The lock names save space at the cost of time since lock headers are dynamically allocated when locks are requested on a lock name. Blocks of lock nodes are allocated to a transaction when it begins, and locks requested by the transaction are quickly allocated from this set.

Lock modes are easily added to the system through the use of two boolean tables, conflicts and covers. The former is obvious, and the second is an optimization which indicates whether a holder of lock type A needs to check for conflicts when requesting a new lock of type B. If A covers B, then this check is unnecessary, since A conflicts with any lock mode B would conflict with.

Locks default to transaction duration, but may be requested for instantaneous duration, operation duration, or *post-commit* duration, in which case they ensure the ability to carry out a post-commit action.

7. Collections and Indexing

The storage allocator provides a low-level interface for allocating and freeing data items. Dalí also provides higher-level interfaces for grouping related data items, and performing scans as well as associative access on data items in a group.

7.1. Heap File

The *heap file* is Dalí's abstraction for handling a large number of fixed-length data items. It is a thin layer provided on top of the power-of-two allocator and the segment headers provided by the allocation system. A separate chunk at the storage allocator level is created for each heap file, and fixed-length items are allocated from segments of the chunk. When creating a heap file, its itemsize – the length of objects in that heap file – is specified. All allocation is done by the underlying allocator, so that the associated logic and concurrency mechanisms are not disturbed. However, it is assumed by the heap file that the underlying allocator will allocate items on exactly itemsize-byte boundries. This is the case with the power-of-two allocator when the minimum allocation size is equal to the fixed size of the items. In addition to insertion and deletion, the heap file supports locking and an unordered scan of items.

Item locking is supported either via lock names (the lock name is derived from the database file and the offset of the item in the database file) or by allocating an array of lock headers for items in each segment. A pointer to this array of lock headers is stored in the segment header, and the page table (described in Section 3.3.2) is used to determine the lock header for an item. Item locks are obtained transparently when items are inserted, deleted, updated or scanned. Responsibility for implementing a lock which covers the entire heap file is *not* implemented in the heap file itself. This corresponds to the principle, which we have encountered repeatedly, that locking for a structure is best left to the encapsulating structure. This has been borne out by very significant difference in the locking needs of the relational and object-oriented databases implemented on Dalí, while the item locking needs are uniformly served by the heap file.

Scans are supported through a bitmap stored in the segment header for items in the segment. Bitmap entries for items that have been deleted from the heap file are 0. Heap file scans thus simply return items in the chunk for which the corresponding bitmap entry is 1. Note that zero entries in the bitmap mirror the allocator's free lists for that segment.

The bitmap makes the process of determining valid records very efficient, and is necessary because information about allocated data is not stored by the allocator due to the implied space overhead for all allocated data.

7.2. *Extendible Hash*

Dalí includes a variation on Extendible Hashing as described in [14]. An overview of our structure appears in Figure 7. The structure matches that of [14], except that the bucket concept from standard extendible hashing is broken into a *hash header* and a list of *key entries*. Thus, each directory entry points to a hash header, and multiple directory entries can point to a single hash header. A variable i is maintained with the hash index, and the first i bits of the computed hash value for a key are used to determine the directory entry for the key (the directory itself contains 2^i entries). Allowing multiple directory entries to point to the same bucket prevents too many hash headers from being allocated for directory entries to which very few key values have hashed. With each hash header is stored a variable j which has the property that for all the keys whose directory entries point to the hash header, the first j bits of their computed hash value are equal. In addition, the number of directory entries that point to the hash header is given by 2^{i-j}.

Searching for a key value is fairly straightforward, and involves searching for the key value in the list of key entries pointed to by the directory entry for the key. Insertions, however, are more complex and could involve splitting individual key entry lists, and in certain cases doubling the entire directory. The algorithm attempts to keep lists below some threshold in size. If an insert pushes a list over the threshold, then that list is *split*. If j in the header for the list to be split is less than i, the list is immediately split into two lists based on the value of the first $j + 1$ bits. Also, the 2^{i-j} entries pointing to the original list are modified to point to one of the two lists based on the first $j + 1$ bits of the hash value the entry represents. After the split, the value of the variable j in the lock headers for the two lists is incremented by 1, and the keys in each list are again equal on the first j bits. Note that j also represents the number of times that the list has split.

The description of splitting above assumed that j in the hash header is less than i for the table. If it is found that j in that list's hash header is equal to i for the hash table then only one entry in the directory points to this list. In this case, a split requires that the directory structure be doubled in size. Our algorithm will forego this split, tolerating somewhat longer lists, until the *utilization factor* (keys/lists) of the hash table has exceeded a certain threshold. Once the threshold has been exceeded, the first attempted split that finds $j = i$ will double the directory structure, and then proceed with the split as above. Other lists whose length exceeds the threshold will be split by the next insert on that list.

The first step in doubling the directory is to allocate a new directory structure twice the size of the original. Directory entries in the new directory that are equal for the first i bits are set to point to the hash header pointed to by the directory entry in the old directory with the same value for the first i bits. The variable i is then incremented (and the original split is carried out). Deletes could similarly cause lists to be merged and possibly the directory size to be halved.

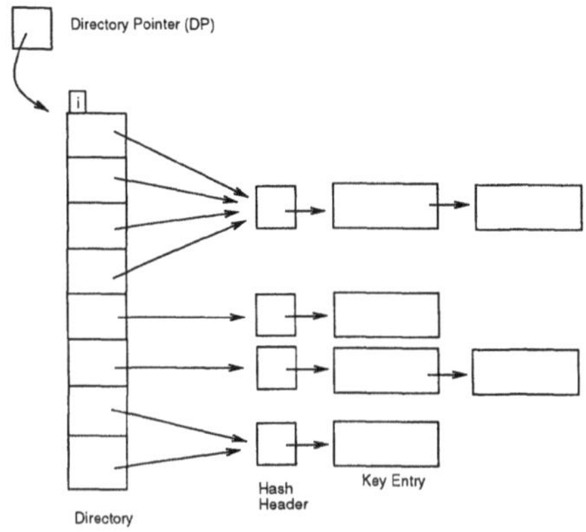

Figure 7. Extendible Hashing in Dalí

In the original proposal, the goal of the work was to provide fast location of records in a disk file. The "directory" size varied linearly with the number of keys in the table, while providing a guaranteed maximum of two disk reads. A similar approach may be worthwhile in main-memory, since keeping space overhead in line with usage is very important, as is speed of access. The cost of accessing a record consists of the cost of navigating the directory structure, followed by key comparisons between the search key and any keys on the overflow chain pointed to by the directory.

Other than our work, [3] describes a variation of extendible hashing for main memory which is related to constructing a trie on the hash value rather than having a single large table. This more complicated scheme significantly decreases space overhead, while keeping a single key compare to determine if the correct record has been found.

In contrast, we maintain the simple directory structure of [14], but avoid the space problems of this scheme by not splitting the structure on overflow of a single bucket. In [14], fixed bucket sizes were implied by disk page sizes, and exceeding this limit triggered the doubling of the directory. In fact, we do not use a fixed size bucket at all, but have a chain of key values for each bucket. We keep space overhead lower by basing the decision to double the directory size on an approximation of occupancy rather than on the local overflow of a bucket.

The advantage of a simple directory structure arises when implementing a concurrency control mechanism. While our implementation may suffer more key comparisons (which may or may not be more expensive than index node traversals in a main memory database), the flat directory structure leads to a simple concurrency control mechanism which nevertheless provides good concurrency.

Permitting insert, delete and find operations to execute concurrently could result in several problems. For example, suppose find for a key causes it to reach a hash header which is split due to a concurrently executing insert. In such a case, the key being searched for may be transferred from the current list to a different list, and find would not be able to locate the key. In order to prevent the above problem, a lock is maintained with each hash header, and two directory locks, the find-directory-lock and the split-directory-lock, are maintained. The directory locks are obtained in exclusive mode when the directory is resized; the split-directory-lock is held while the new directory is being initialized while the find-directory-lock is held only when the pointer to the directory is toggled to point to the new larger directory.

Operator find begins by first obtaining the find-directory-lock in shared mode – this ensures that the directory stays stable during the find operation. It then obtains a lock on the hash header. Furthermore, in order to ensure that the hash header has not been split between the time it reached the hash header and the time it obtained a shared lock on it, it checks to see if the directory entry that initially pointed to its hash header is still unchanged. If this is the case, find can release the find-directory-lock and proceed; else, it releases the lock on the hash header and re-traverses the directory structure to reach the correct hash header. Operator insert, on the other hand, obtains the hash header lock in exclusive mode. If it is decided to split the header, then a shared lock is obtained on the split-directory-lock to ensure that the directory is not being resized while the split is taking place. Since splits are an optimization, an insert may choose not to wait if this lock is held, allowing the next insert to perform the split.

Note that maintaining the find and split directory locks as separate locks ensures that find operations and normal insert operations (those that do not cause splits) are only blocked for the very short time required to toggle the directory pointer when a directory is being resized. Since the split-directory-lock is acquired in exclusive mode for the duration of the doubling, it ensures that two processes do not try to double the directory at the same time. Note that if a process cannot get this lock, it simply gives up, since another process is already accomplishing the doubling.

7.3. T-tree Indexes

In [29], the authors proposed T-trees as a storage efficient data structure for main memory databases. T-trees are based on AVL trees proposed in [2]. In this subsection, we provide an overview of T-trees as implemented in Dalí. For a detailed description, the reader is referred to [8].

7.3.1. Overview of T-trees

We now describe the T-tree from [29]. Like AVL trees, the height of left and right subtrees of a T-tree may differ by at most one. Unlike AVL trees, each node in a T-tree stores multiple key values in a sorted order, rather than a single key value. The left-most and the right-most key value in a node define the range of key values contained in the node. Thus, the left subtree of a node contains only key values less than the left-most key value, while the right subtree contains key values greater than the right-most key value in the node. A key value which is falls between the smallest and largest key values in a node is said to be *bounded* by that node. Note that keys equal to the smallest or largest key in the node may or may not be considered to be bounded based on whether the index is unique and based on the search condition (e.g. "greater-than" versus "greater-than or equal-to").

A node with both a left and a right child is referred to as an *internal node*, a node with only one child is referred to as a *semi-leaf*, and a node with no children is referred to as a *leaf*. In order to keep occupancy high, every internal node has a minimum number of key values that it must contain (typically $k-2$, if k is the maximum number of keys that can be stored in a node). However, there is no occupancy condition on the leaves or semi-leaves.

Searching for a key value in a T-tree is relatively straightforward. For every node, a check is made to see if the key value is bounded by the left-most and the right-most key value in the node; if this is the case, then the key value is returned if it is contained in the node (else, the key value is not contained in the tree). Otherwise, if the key value is less than the left-most key value, then the left child node is searched; else the right child node is searched. The process is repeated until either the key is found or the node to be searched is null.

Insertions and deletions into the T-tree are a bit more complicated. For insertions, first a variant of the search described above is used to find the node that bounds the key value to be inserted. If such a node exists, then if there is room in the node, the key value is inserted into the node. If there is no room in the node, then the key value is inserted into the node and the left-most key value in the node is inserted into the left subtree of the node (if the left subtree is empty, then a new node is allocated and the left-most key value is inserted into it). If no bounding node is found then let N be the last node encountered by the failed search and proceed as follows: If N has room, the key value is inserted into N; else, it is inserted into a new node that is either the right or left child of N depending on the key value and the left-most and right-most key values in N.

Deletion of a key value begins by determining the node containing the key value, and the key value is deleted from the node. If deleting the key value results in an empty leaf node, then the node is deleted. If the deletion results in an internal node or semi-leaf containing fewer than the minimum number of key values, then the deficit is made up by moving the largest key in the left subtree into the node, or by merging the node with its right child.

In both insert and delete, allocation/de-allocation of a node may cause the tree to become unbalanced and rotations (RR, RL, LL, LR) described in [29] may need to be performed. (The heights of subtrees in the following description include the effects of the insert or delete.) In the case of an insert, nodes along the path from the newly allocated node to the root are examined until either 1) a node for which the two subtrees have equal heights is found (in this case no rotation needs to be performed), or 2) a node for which the difference in heights between the left and the right subtrees is more than one is found and a single rotation involving the node is performed. In the case of delete, nodes along the path from the de-allocated node's parent to the root are examined until a node is found whose subtrees' heights now differ by one. Furthermore, every time a node whose subtrees' heights differ by more than one is encountered, a rotation is performed. Note that de-allocation of a node may result in multiple rotations.

7.3.2. Concurrency control Issues in T-trees

We now describe the features of our implementation of T-trees in Dalí. We implement T-trees with a single tree latch which is obtained in shared mode for readers and exclusive mode for updaters. In our implementation, each node contains a *version number* which is incremented whenever the node is modified. Also, a stack is used for all operations on the T-tree. The stack stores the nodes visited during a traversal, whether the left or right child was taken when leaving the node, and the version number of the node when it was first encountered. In the following, a version number is said to have *changed* if the current version number in the node is different from the version number stored in the stack.

Our T-tree implementation supports next-key-locking [37, 35] to avoid the *phantom phenomenon* (see e.g. [24]). Thus, in our implementation, a key in the range of an in-progress scan cannot be inserted or deleted since this could result in a non-serializable execution. This is controlled by passing lock modes to each operation, so that transactions running at lower degrees of consistency can be mixed with those running at higher degrees [17].

Even though search operations on T-trees obtain the tree latch, concurrent inserters and deleters could cause problems. For example, consider searching for a key greater than a certain value. Once the target key has been found, a lock on it needs to be obtained. However, the lock request cannot be made while holding the latch since this could result in deadlocks involving latches and locks. As a result, the latch must be released before the lock request is made – this, however, opens up a window for inserters who could insert a key value in between the value being searched for and the target key determined by the search procedure. Thus, after the lock is obtained, the search procedure needs to perform a *validation* to ensure that the target key has not been invalidated due to a concurrently executing insert or delete.

In general, the search proceeds as described in Section 7.3.1 except that each node visited is pushed onto the stack. We describe only the search for a "greater-than" value, though all comparisons are supported in the implementation. After a lock on the target key is obtained, validation is performed. Let N be the top node on the stack (which is the last node seen in the search), and let search value be the key value on which the search was initiated and target value the key value locked just prior to the validation. Then validation is said to succeed if any of the following is true.

1. Search value is bounded by N, and either the version number of N is unchanged or N does not contain a key value between search value and target value.
2. Search value is less than the smallest key in N, and the version number of N has not changed, and N has no left child (thus, no new key between search value and target value could have been inserted, and target value itself, could not have been deleted).
3. Search value is greater than largest key in N, and the version number of N has not changed, and N has no right child.

In case validation fails, the lock on the target key is released and the search is resumed from the most recently visited node in the stack whose version number is the same as that noted in the stack. The intuition for this is based on the observation that no target key could "escape" from a subtree without modifying, and therefore changing the version number of the root of that subtree. Note that restarting as described above implies that termination of the algorithm is probabilistic, but this is true of every scheme that follows the unlatch-lock-validate model [35, 37]. Successive key values in a range are obtained by repeatedly invoking the search procedure with the key value returned by the previous invocation and the stack at the end of the previous search.

Inserts and deletes on the T-tree are implemented as described in the overview above. Inserts on the tree invoke the search procedure to obtain a short duration (exclusive lock) lock on the key value larger than the key being inserted to ensure that no scans are in progress (this is referred to as next-key locking [35]). Once this is done, modifications to T-tree nodes and rotations are performed while holding the T-tree latch in exclusive mode. Updates also increment the version number for any node which has been changed (note, however, that changing balance information does not require changing the version number). Deletes, on the other hand, obtain an additional transaction duration lock on the key value larger than the key value being deleted. This lock (combined with next-key locking on inserts) ensures the ability to abort the transaction by reinserting the missing key, and also prevent scans from proceeding past the deleted key, avoiding the phantom problem. Once this next-key lock is acquired which, the key delete on the node is performed while holding the T-tree latch in exclusive mode. Both inserts and deletes on the T-tree are treated as operations and multi-level recovery techniques described in Section 4 are employed for maintaining consistency in the presence of system crashes. For example, the undo operation for an insert is a delete, but any rotations caused by the insert are not necessarily undone by the delete (though new rotations may be caused).

8. Higher level Interfaces

There are currently two database management systems built on the Dalí Storage Manager. The Dalí Relational Manager is a C++ class library interface built on the relational model. This product retains the name Dalí, following our principle of offering multiple levels of interface. The second database management system built on Dalí is a main memory version of the ODE Object-Oriented Database. MM-ODE includes a compiler (O++) which supports a small superset of the C++ syntax. We now provide a brief overview of these high-level interfaces to Dalí.

8.1. Dali Relational Manager

The Dalí Relational Manager is a C++ class library interface to a relational system with SQL support limited to definition statements. Access to data is through C++ classes, corresponding to tables, iterators, search criteria, etc. Schema information is stored in tables, and limited views (projection only) are allowed. Indices may be created on arbitrary subsets of the attributes in a table. Referential integrity is supported (foreign key constraints), as are null values. Locking strategies avoid "phantom" anomalies (see e.g. [24]).

Navigation is supported through iterators over a single table. A conjunctive query may be specified for the iterator, and automatic index selection is performed.

The one extension to the relational model is that inter-table joins may be stored in the schema. From one open iterator, a new iterator on the matching tuples in the other table may easily be opened. This join relationship may be *materialized* leading to underlying pointer list structures similar to a network database. This last feature is required for the relational interface to allow navigation which competes with object-oriented models without explicit pointer types.

Building this interface has served the dual purposes of providing a higher-level interface for users and serving as a validation of the storage manager functionality. The interface described here took approximately one staff-year to produce, which we feel is very reasonable for a full-featured system, and illustrates the leverage gained from a good storage manager.

8.2. MM-Ode Object Oriented Database

MM-Ode<Dali>, also known as MM-Ode, is the main-memory version of the Ode object-oriented database system. It is built using the Dali main memory storage manager. MM-Ode supports a user interface identical to that provided by Ode<EOS>, also known as Ode, an object database described in [1, 4, 32] The primary interface for both database management systems is the database programming language O++, which is based on C++. A few facilities have been added to C++ to make it suitable for database applications. O++ provides facilities for creating persistent objects which are stored in the database and for querying the database by iterating over these objects. Navigation is supported through pointers to persistent objects. It also has support for versioned objects. Indexes can also be built to speed-up object access. The run-time system checks for the existence of an index relevant to each query that may benefit from index use. The most recent release of MM-Ode allows triggers to be associated with objects.[8] Use of Ode allows applications to be used on both a disk-based (Ode) and a main-memory (MM-Ode) database. Recompilation is the only porting effort required. MM-Ode programs are often significantly shorter and easier-to-understand than the corresponding Dali program. However, this convenience comes at a significant performance cost. We are looking into reducing these costs.

9. Conclusion

We have presented a detailed overview of the architecture of the Dalí Main-Memory Storage Manager. To our knowledge, Dalí is the only main-memory storage manager tuned for fine-grained concurrency and small transactions. Also, to our knowledge, it is the only explicit implementation of multi-level recovery for main-memory, and one of very few for disk-based systems. We have described the storage architecture for Dalí, and the implementation of the T-tree and extendible hash index structures. We have presented an overview of our multi-level concurrency control and recovery services, and described how the design of these services allows for minimal conflict with running transactions – in particular through the use of fuzzy checkpoints and through techniques for physical versioning of index structures.

We have also described the extensive features for detection of bad writes by processes, and for recovery from process failure. We have briefly described the two database managment systems currently built on Dalí, the Dalí Relation Manager, and the MM-Ode main-memory object-oriented database.

With the exception of the extendible hash, which is actively being added to the system at this time, all features of the design described here are implemented in the current version of Dalí at Bell Laboratories. Our future work includes logical versioning at the relational level, and data-shipping distributed versions based on the shared disk or client-server model.

Acknowledgements

We would like to thank H. V. Jagadish for significant early contributions to Dalí. Steve Coomer suggested the strategy of using codewords to protect checkpoint images on disk. Dennis Leinbaugh suggested the structure of the free tree. We would like to thank Jerry Baulier for his support of the project. We would also like to thank the following talented individuals who have contributed to design and implementation of specific systems in Dalí over the last three years: Soumya Chakraborty, Ajay Deshpande, Sadanand Gogate, Chandra Gupta, Sandeep Joshi, Amit Khivesara, Sekhara Muddana, Mike Nemeth, James Parker, and Yogesh Wagle.

Notes

1. Named in honor of Salvadore Dalí, for his famous painting, "The Persistence of Memory".
2. For some of the interfaces, a copying mode is also supported.
3. For more information, see `http://www.bell-labs.com/org/1123/what/dali/`
4. System M [39] is a transaction processing test-bed for memory resident data, but is not a full featured storage manager.
5. The database here represents a single database file. In fact, different database files can be checkpointed at different times, and transactions can span database files arbitrarily. The generalization for multiple database files is straightforward, but is omitted for clarity and space.
6. In cases when region sizes change, certain additional region locks on storage allocation structures may need to be obtained. For example, in a page-based system, if an update causes the size of a tuple to change, then in addition to a region lock on the tuple, an X mode region lock on the storage allocation structures on the page must be obtained.
7. These are stored with the process rather than the transaction to handle very low level latches, such as the one used to allocate transaction table entries.
8. More information on the MM-Ode Object Oriented Database may be obtained on the World-Wide Web at `http://www-db.research.bell-labs.com/ode-announce.univ.html`.

References

1. R. Agrawal and N. Gehani, "Ode (object database and environment): the language and the data model," in Proc. of ACM-SIGMOD Int'l Conference on Management of Data, Portland, OR, May 1989, pp. 36–45.
2. A. Aho, J. Hopcroft, and J. D. Ullman, The Design and Analysis of Computer Algorithms, Addison-Wesley, 1974.

3. A. Analyti and S. Pramanik, "Fast search in main memory databases," in Proc. of ACM-SIGMOD Int'l Conference on Management of Data, 1992.
4. R. Arlein, J. Gava, N. Gehani, and D. Lieuwen, Ode 4.2 user manual, Included in distribution at `ftp://research.att.com/dist/ode/doc`, 1996.
5. D. Batory, J. Barnett, J. Garza, K. Smith, K. Tsukuda, B. Twichell, and T. Wise, "Genesis: An extensible database management system," in S. Zdonik and D. Maier, editors, Readings in Object-Oriented Database Systems, Morgan Kaufman, 1990.
6. P.A. Bernstein, M. Hsu, and B. Mann, "Implementing recoverable requests using queues," in Proc. of ACM-SIGMOD Int'l Conference on Management of Data, May 1990.
7. A. Biliris and E. Panagos, EOS User's Guide, Release 2.0.0, Technical report, AT&T Bell Labs, 1993, BL011356-930505-25M.
8. P. Bohannon, D. Leinbaugh, R. Rastogi, S. Seshadri, A. Silberschatz, and S. Sudarshan, Logical and physical versioning in main memory databases, Technical Report 113880-951031-12, Lucent Technologies Bell Laboratories, Murray Hill, 1995.
9. P. Bohannon, D. Lieuwen, A. Silbershatz, S. Sudarshan, and J. Gava, "Recoverable user-level mutual exclusion," in Proc. 7th IEEE Symposium on Parallel and Distributed Processing, October 1995.
10. P. Bohannon, J. Parker, R. Rastogi, S. Seshadri, A. Silberschatz, and S. Sudarshan, Distributed multi-level recovery in main memory databases, Technical Report 1125300-96-0227-01TM, Lucent Technologies Bell Laboratories, Murray Hill, 1996.
11. M. J. Carey, D. J. DeWitt, J. E. Richardson, and E. J. Shekita, "Storage management for objects in EXODUS," in W. Kim and F. H. Lochovsky, editors, Object-Oriented Concepts and Databases, Addison-Wesley, 1989.
12. D. J. DeWitt, R. Katz, F. Olken, D. Shapiro, M. Stonebraker, and D. Wood, "Implementation techniques for main memory database systems," in Proc. of ACM-SIGMOD Int'l Conference on Management of Data, Boston, Mass., June 1984, pp. 1–8.
13. M.H. Eich, "A classification and comparison of main memory database recovery techniques," in Proc. of the IEEE Conference on Data Engineering, Los Angeles, CA, February 1989, pp. 332.
14. R. Fagin, J. Nievergelt, N. Pippenger, and H.R. Strong, Extendible hashing — a fast access method for dynamic files, IBM, Res.R. RJ2305, July 1978.
15. H. Garcia-Molina and K. Salem, "Main memory database systems: An overview," IEEE Transactions on Knowledge and Data Engineering, Vol. 4, pp. 509–516, 1992.
16. V. Gottemukkala and T. Lehman, "Locking and latching in a memory-resident database system," in Proc. of the Int'l Conf. on Very Large Databases, August 1992, pp. 533–544.
17. J. N. Gray, R. A. Lorie, G. F. Putzolu, and I. L. Traiger., "Granularity of locks and degrees of consistency in a shared database," in G.M. Nijssen, editor, Modeling in Data Base Management Systems, pp. 365–394. North-Holland, Amsterdam, 1976.
18. L. M. Haas, W. Chang, G. M. Lohman, J. McPherson, P. F. Wilms, G. Lapis, B. Lindsay, H. Pirahesh, M. Carey, and E. Shekita, Starburst mid-flight: As the dust clears," IEEE Transactions on Knowledge and Data Engineering, Vol. 2, March 1990.
19. Robert B. Hagmann, "A crash recovery scheme for a memory-resident database system," IEEE Transactions on Computers, Vol. C-35, pp. 839–847, 1986.
20. Maruice Herlihy, "A methodology for implementing highly concurrent data structures," in ACM SIGPLAN Symp. on Principles and Practice of Parallel Programming, March 1989.
21. Maurice Herlihy, Impossibility and universality results for wait-free synchronization, Technical report, CMU, TR-CS-88-140, May 1988.
22. H. V. Jagadish, Dan Lieuwen, Rajeev Rastogi, Avi Silberschatz, and S. Sudarshan, "Dali: A high performance main-memory storage manager," in Proc. of the Int'l Conf. on Very Large Databases, 1994.
23. H. V. Jagadish, Avi Silberschatz, and S. Sudarshan, "Recovering from main-memory lapses," in Proc. of the Int'l Conf. on Very Large Databases, 1993.
24. H. Korth and A. Silberschatz, Database System Concepts. McGraw-Hill, (second edition), 720pp., 1991.
25. H. T. Kung and P. L. Lehman, "Concurrent manipulation of binary search trees," ACM Transactions on Database Systems, Vol. 5, pp. 354–382, 1980.
26. Charles Lamb, Gordon Landis, Jack Orenstein, and Dan Weinreb, "The ObjectStore database system," CACM, Vol. 34, pp. 50–63, 1991.
27. T. Lehman, E. J. Shekita, and L. Cabrera, "An evaluation of Starburst's memory resident storage component," IEEE Transactions on Knowledge and Data Engineering, Vol. 4, 1992, pp. 555–566.

28. T. J. Lehman and M. J. Carey, "Query processing in main memory database management system," in Proc. of ACM-SIGMOD Int'l Conference on Management of Data, pp. 239–250, 1986.
29. T. J. Lehman and M. J. Carey, "A study of index structures for main memory database management systems," in Proc. of the Int'l Conf. on Very Large Databases, August 1986, pp. 294–303.
30. T. J. Lehman and M. J. Carey, "A recovery algorithm for a high-performance memory-resident database system," in Proc. of ACM-SIGMOD Int'l Conference on Management of Data, 1987, pp. 104–117.
31. X. Li and M. Eich, "Post-crash log processing for fuzzy checkpointing main memory databases," in Proc. IEEE CS Intl. Conf. on Data Engineering, April 1993.
32. Daniel F. Lieuwen, Narain Gehani, , and Robert Arlein, "The Ode active database: Trigger semantics and implementation," in Proc. Data Engineering, February–March 1996.
33. D. Lomet, "MLR: A recovery method for multi-level systems," in Proc. of ACM-SIGMOD Int'l Conference on Management of Data, 1992, pp. 185–194.
34. U. Manber and G. D. Ladner, "Concurrency control in dynamic search structures," ACM Proc.on Database Systems, April 1982, pp. 268–282.
35. C. Mohan, "ARIES/KVL: A key-value locking method for concurrency control of multiaction transactions operating on Btree indexes," In IBM Almaden Res.Ctr, Res.R. No.RJ7008, 27pp., March 1990.
36. C. Mohan, D. Haderle, B. Lindsay, H. Pirahesh, and P. Schwarz, "ARIES: A transaction recovery method supporting fine-granularity locking and partial rollbacks using write-ahead logging," ACM Transactions on Database Systems, Vol. 17, pp. 94–162, 1992.
37. C. Mohan and F. Levine, "ARIES/IM an efficient and high concurrency index management method using write-ahead logging," in Proc. of ACM-SIGMOD Int'l Conference on Management of Data, June 1992.
38. B. Özden, R. Rastogi, A. Silberschatz, P. S. Nararyan, and C. Martin, "The Fellini multimedia storage server," In S. M. Chung, editor, Multimedia Information Storage and Management, Kluwer Academic Publishers, 1996.
39. K. Salem and H. Garcia-Molina, "System M: A transaction processing testbed for memory resident data," IEEE Transactions on Knowledge and Data Engineering, Vol. 2, pp. 161–172, March 1990.
40. E. Shekita and M. Zwilling, "Cricket: A Mapped Persistent Object Store," in Proc. of the Persistent Object Systems Workshop, Martha's Vineyard, MA, September 1990.
41. V. Singhal, S. V. Kakkad, and P. R. Wilson, "Texas: An efficient, portable persistent store," in Proc. Fifth Int'l. Workshop on Persistent Object Systems, September 1992.
42. Mark Sullivan and Michael Stonebreaker, "Using write protected data structures to improve software fault tolerance in highly available database management systems," in Proc. of the Int'l Conf. on Very Large Databases, 1991, pp. 171–179.
43. J. Turek, D. Shasha, and S. Prakash, "Locking without blocking: Making lock based concurrent data structure algorithms nonblocking," in Proc. of the ACM SIGACT-SIGMOD-SIGART Symposium on Principles of Database Systems, June 1992.
44. G. Weikum, C. Hasse, P. Broessler, and P. Muth, "Multi-level recovery," in Proc. of the ACM SIGACT-SIGMOD-SIGART Symposium on Principles of Database Systems, June 1990, pp. 109–123.
45. Seth J. White and David J. DeWitt, "Quickstore: A high performance mapped object store, in Proc. of ACM-SIGMOD Int'l Conference on Management of Data, 1994.

Philip Bohannon received a B.S. in Computer Science from Birmingham-Southern College in 1986. He is a Ph.D. candidate working in database management and transaction processing at Rutgers University. He has been working with the Dali project at Bell Laboratories for the last 3 years.

Daniel F. Lieuwen is a member of technical staff in the Database Systems Research Department at Bell Laboratories, Murray Hill, NJ. His main research focus has been on object-oriented databases (particularly Ode), main-memory databases, and active databases, but he is currently branching out into topics related to materialized views and databases-on-the-web. Mr. Lieuwen attended Calvin College, Grand Rapids, Michigan where he studied mathematics and computer science (and a fair bit of German). He received the M.S. and Ph.D. degrees in Computer Science from the University of Wisconsin-Madison. He joined Bell Laboratories in 1992.

Rajeev Rastogi is a member of technical staff at AT&T Bell laboratories, where he works in the areas of database systems and file systems. His technical interests include high-performance transaction processing, fault-tolerant storage managers and multimedia file systems. He graduated with a B. Tech degree in computer science from the Indian Institute of Technology at Bombay in 1988, and with MS and Phd degrees in computer science (1990 and 1993, respectively) from the University of Texas at Austin.

Abraham Silberschatz (Ph.D. the State University of New York at Stony Brook) is the director of the Information Sciences Research Center at Bell Laboratories, Murray Hill, New Jersey. Prior to joining Bell Labs, he was an endowed professor in the Department of Computer Sciences at the University of Texas at Austin. Professor Silberschatz is a recognized researcher, educator, and author. His research interest include database systems, operating systems, and distributed systems. His writings have appeared in numerous ACM and IEEE publications and he is co-author of two well known textbooks – Operating System Concepts and Database System Concepts. Dr. Silberschatz is a Fellow of the ACM.

S. Seshadri is currently an Assistant Professor in the Computer Science and Engineering Department of IIT Bombay. He obtained his B.Tech from IIT Madras in 1988, MS from University of Wisconsin-Madison in 1990 and Ph.D from University of Wisconsin-Madison in 1992. His research interests are in the areas of: main memory database systems, object oriented database systems, parallel database systems, transaction management and complex query processing.

S. Sudarshan did his B.Tech. from the Indian Institute of Technology, Madras in 1987, and his Ph.D. from the University of Wisconsin, in 1992, both in Computer Science. He was a member of the technical staff in the database research group in Bell Laboratories from 1992 to 1995, and has been on the faculty at the Indian Institute of Technology, Bombay since. His research interests are in database systems, concentrating in the areas of query processing, particularly processing of complex queries, and recovery and failure resilience issues in main memory database systems.

Multimedia Tools and Applications, 4, 153–170 (1997)

Supporting Content-Based Retrieval in Large Image Database Systems

EDWARD REMIAS
Department of Electrical and Computer Engineering, State University of New York at Buffalo, Buffalo, NY 14260

GHOLAMHOSEIN SHEIKHOLESLAMI, AIDONG ZHANG azhang@cs.buffalo.edu
Department of Computer Science State University of New York at Buffalo, Buffalo, NY 14260

TANVEER FATHIMA SYEDA-MAHMOOD
Xerox Research Center, Webster, NY 14580

Abstract. In this paper, we investigate approaches to supporting effective and efficient retrieval of image data based on content. We first introduce an effective block-oriented image decomposition structure which can be used to represent image content in image database systems. We then discuss the application of this image data model to content-based image retrieval. Using wavelet transforms to extract image features, significant content features can be extracted from image data through decorrelating the data in their pixel format into frequency domain. Feature vectors of images can then be constructed. Content-based image retrieval is performed by comparing the feature vectors of the query image and the decomposed segments in database images. Our experimental analysis illustrates that the proposed block-oriented image representation offers a novel decomposition structure to be used to facilitate effective and efficient image retrieval.

Keywords: content-based image retrieval, image database systems, texture, image decomposition, image representation, wavelet transforms

1. Introduction

Content-based image retrieval has been proposed to allow retrievals to be performed on the basis of a variety of aspects of image content [1, 5, 15, 10, 6, 2, 18]. In this context, a challenging problem arises with many image databases, within which queries are posed via visual or pictorial examples. We term such queries *visual queries*. A common visual query to an image database system would involve finding all images in that database which contain a subimage that is similar to a given query image. Such retrievals must use embedded content features, such as the shape, color, texture, layout, and position of various objects in an image. There have not been generic tools which can facilitate to understand image content to a satisfiable extent. The automatic retrieval of images on the basis of content thus pose difficult problems. An approach which has drawn much recent attention involves the extraction of the color and texture features of images using image processing techniques. Currently, most research proposes to formulate image feature vectors based on color and texture characteristics. Content-based image retrieval is then supported by searching and comparing the feature vectors of the query image and database images.

As the feature vector of a database image may not correctly represent its subimages, the retrieval based on the comparison between the feature vectors of the query image and database images themselves may not provide satisfiable results for visual queries. Thus, image segmentation is necessary in the implementation of feature-based techniques for searching image databases [11]. Effective segmentation will isolate the important features of the images in the database. Ideally, the results generated through the process of image recognition and analysis would be used to automatically segment image content. However, as image recognition itself is still in its formative stage, investigations in this direction are still in their infancy. To avoid manual segmentation of images in a large image database, a block-oriented approach based on quad-tree decomposition of images has been adopted to circumvent the difficulty of automatic segmentation [5, 11]. An effective query-by-texture approach using quad-tree segmentation and wavelet transforms has been presented [11]. The decomposition approach was demonstrated to be effective.

In this paper, we conduct a comprehensive study on image data representation and retrieval approaches to support effective and efficient retrieval of image data based on content. We first introduce an effective block-oriented image decomposition structure to be used in content-based image retrieval. This structure is an extension of the quad-tree decomposition. We then discuss the application of this data model to content-based image retrieval. Wavelet transforms are used to extract image features. Significant content features are extracted from image data in their pixel format through decorrelating the image data into frequency domain using wavelets. Feature vectors of images can then be constructed. Content-based image retrieval is performed by comparing the feature vectors of the query image and the segments in database images. Our experimental analysis illustrates that the nona-tree decomposition offers a novel decomposition structure to be used to facilitate effective and efficient image retrieval.

The rest of the paper is organized as follows. Section 2 introduces the block-oriented data structure, namely, nona-tree, and discusses the computational complexity of this data structure. Section 3 investigates the application of the nona-tree image representation in content-based image retrieval. Experimental results will be presented in this section. Section 4 offers discussions on the effectiveness of the nona-tree decomposition with different wavelet transforms and compares the effectiveness of the nona-tree decomposition with other block-oriented decomposition approaches. Concluding remarks are offered in Section 5.

2. Image Data Modeling — Nona-trees

In this section, we will present the nona-tree image decomposition structure to be used to specify image content in image databases. We then discuss the computational complexity of the nona-tree decomposition structure.

2.1. Nona-tree

A *nona-tree* is a hierarchical image decomposition structure based on a slight modification of the recursive decomposition of images that is proposed in quad-trees [4]. That is, each decomposition on an image segment produces nine subsegments of equal size rather than four. These subsegments include four equal-sized quadrants (numbered 1, 2, 3, and 4), one subsegment of the same size as each quadrant taken from the central area of the image segment (numbered 5) , and four subsegments of the same size as each quadrant produced from the central areas of the upper, bottom, left, and right halves of the image segment (numbered 6, 7, 8 and 9). Figure 1 demonstrates the positions of these subsegments in the decomposed image segment.

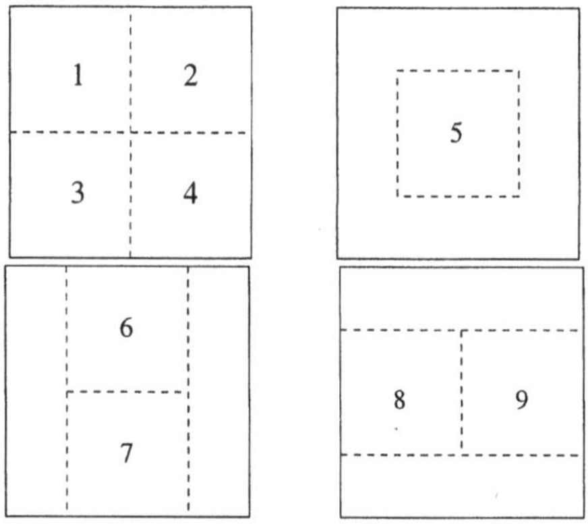

Figure 1. Nine subsegments in nona-tree decomposition.

The decomposition process of a nona-tree can be described recursively with the root representing the entire image and its children representing the decomposed segments which, in turn, are roots for further decomposed segments. Each internal node has at most nine children. The strategy of quad-tree decomposition proposed in [11] can be used in determining the decomposition of subsegments 1, 2, 3 and 4 in the nona-tree. That is, decompositions are only carried out on the segments with heterogeneous textures. Before four children are spawned by each parent, conditions for merging are tested. A distance threshold is computed for each child on the basis of extracted texture features. The distances in the feature space are measured from the parent node to each child. If the distances to all four children fall within the thresholds of the children, a single texture would be declared in the parent node, and no further decomposition is necessary. Otherwise, pair-wise grouping of the children will then be performed. That is, if the distance between two neighboring children falls below the thresholds of both, the children are merged as a single child. Also, whether or not the subsegments 1, 2, 3 and 4 are generated determines the generation of subsegment 5, 6, 7 and 8. We have the following cases:

- *No decomposition of subsegments 1, 2, 3, and 4*: a single texture has been declared for the segment. Thus, subsegment 5, 6, 7, 8, and 9 should not be generated.
- *No decomposition of subsegments 1 and 2*: a single texture has been declared for the merging of subsegments 1 and 2. Thus, subsegment 6 should not be generated.
- *No decomposition of subsegments 1 and 3*: a single texture has been declared for the merging of subsegments 1 and 3. Thus, subsegment 8 should not be generated.

- *No decomposition of subsegments 2 and 4*: a single texture has been declared for the merging of subsegments 2 and 4. Thus, subsegment 9 should not be generated.
- *No decomposition of subsegments 3 and 4*: a single texture has been declared for the merging of subsegments 3 and 4. Thus, subsegment 7 should not be generated.

Those subsegments which do not correspond to any of the above cases are generated in the nona-tree. Figure 2 illustrates the representation of an image by a nona-tree data structure in which the subsegments of each segment are listed in the increasingly numbering order. For example, at the first level of decomposition, the given image is decomposed into nine segments. All segments are heterogeneous and thus further decomposition is needed. At the second level of decomposition, segment 2 obtained from the first level is decomposed into nine subsegments. In this decomposition, subsegments 1, 2, 4, 6 and 9 are homogeneous and all other subsegments are heterogeneous. Other segments can be similarly decomposed.

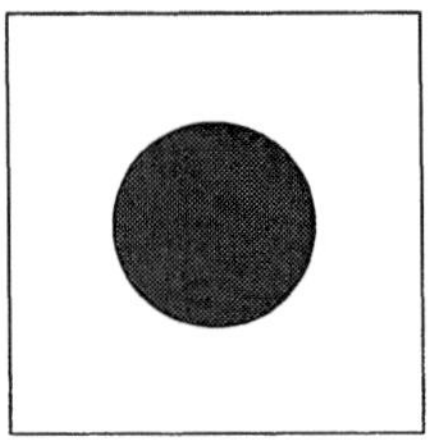

(a)

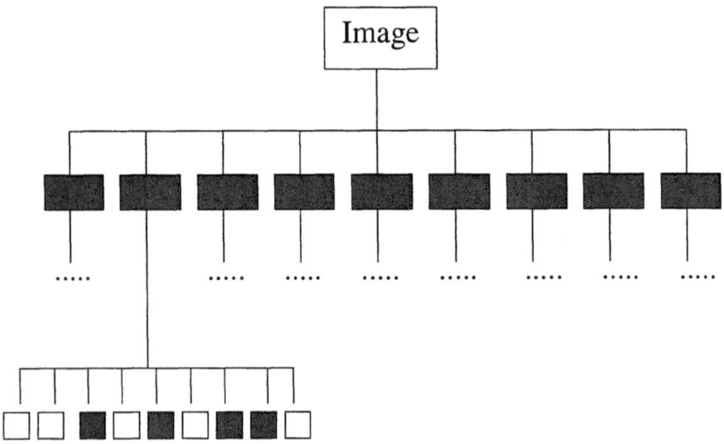

(b)

Figure 2. (a) Image; (b) Nona-tree.

2.2. *Computational Analysis*

We now discuss the maximum number of segments existing in a nona-tree and analyze the overlapping coverage between a query image and the segments of a database image in the situation of the query image is similar to a subimage of the database image.

2.2.1. *Number of Segments in Nona-tree*

Table 1 illustrates the relationship between image size and nona-tree level.

Table 1. Nona-tree level and image size in the hierarchy

Level	0	1	2	3	4
Image Size	256x256	128x128	64x64	32x32	16x16

We will now discuss the maximum number of segments existing in a nona-tree with i levels. Clearly, at each level i, there are at most 9^i possible segments. However, there are redundant segments; these start at level two of the nona-tree. We introduce the concept of a *representative point* for each segment to illustrate the maximum number of segments possible in each nona-tree. The representative point of a segment in a nona-tree refers to the uppermost left point of that segment. Thus, in Figure 3 (a), labeled bold points A through I are representative points for the nine subsegments of the given segment. That is, points A, C, G, I in Figure 3 (a) are representative points for subsegments 1, 2, 3, 4, respectively. Point E represents subsegment 5, and points B, H, D, F represent subsegments 6, 7, 8, 9, respectively. Thus, at level 1, we have $3 \times 3 = (2^2 - 1) \times (2^2 - 1)$ segments, which is 9. Subsegments at the next level are similarly labeled in Figure 3 (b). Note that some of the points represent multiple segments. For example, the point labeled N in Figure 3 (b) represents the shaded area which appears to be a subsegment of segment 1, 5, 6, and 8 at level 1. This subsegment is the fourth subsegment of segment 1, the first subsegment of segment 5, the third subsegment of segment 6, and the second subsegment of segment 8. In Figure 3 (b), there are actually $7 \times 7 = 49$ rather than $9^2 = 81$ subsegments at the third level of the nona-tree, which can also be expressed as $(2^3 - 1) \times (2^3 - 1)$. Thus, there are $81 - 49 = 32$ redundant subsegments. By analyzing these numbers, at the ith level, we have at most $(2^{i+1} - 1)^2$ instead of 9^i subsegments. Table 2 lists the maximum number of segments at each level of a nona-tree.

Thus, strictly speaking, nona-trees are hierarchical graphs in which nodes in different branches at one level may share common nodes at the next lower level.

Table 2. Maximum number of segments in nona-tree

Level	i	0	1	2	3	4
segments in nona-tree	$(2^{i+1} - 1)^2$	1	9	49	225	961

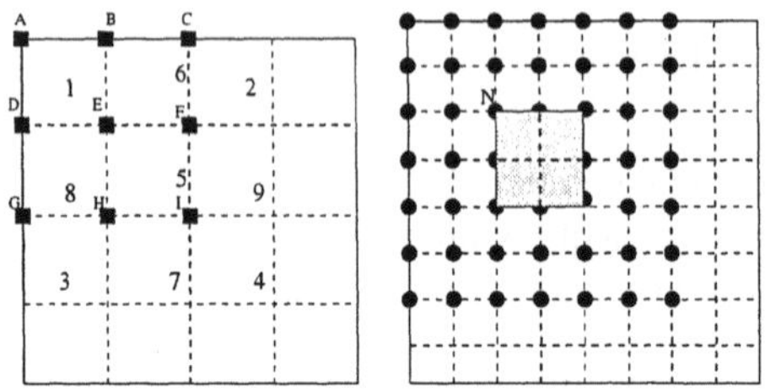

(a) (b)

Figure 3. (a) Segment decomposition and representative points at level 1; (b) Segment decomposition and representative points at level 2.

2.2.2. *Subimage Coverage*

The nona-tree decomposition ensures that, if a portion of a decomposed image matches a query image, there then exists a segment which covers at least $\frac{9}{16}$ of the query image. Figure 4 illustrates the situation. In this example, we assume that the size of the query image is compatible with that of the first level decomposition. In Figure 4 (a), the shaded area of the query image is $(\frac{3}{4}r)^2$, which is $\frac{9}{16}r^2$. In general, as shown in Figure 4 (b), the covered area A of the query image has the following cases:

- $r_1, r_2 \le \frac{1}{4}r$: the area covered by segment 5 is:

$$A = (r - r_1) \times (r - r_2) \ge \frac{9}{16}r^2.$$

- $r_1 \le \frac{1}{4}r$ and $r_2 \ge \frac{1}{4}r$: the area covered by segment 6 is:

$$A = (r - r_1) \times (\frac{1}{2}r + r_2) \ge \frac{9}{16}r^2.$$

- $r_1 \ge \frac{1}{4}r$ and $r_2 \le \frac{1}{4}r$: the area covered by segment 8 is:

$$A = (r - r_2) \times (\frac{1}{2}r + r_1) \ge \frac{9}{16}r^2.$$

- $r_1, r_2 \ge \frac{1}{4}r$: the area covered by segment 1 is:

$$A = (\frac{1}{2}r + r_1) \times (\frac{1}{2}r + r_2) \ge \frac{9}{16}r^2.$$

Clearly, this also holds when the query image is located in other places within the decomposed image.

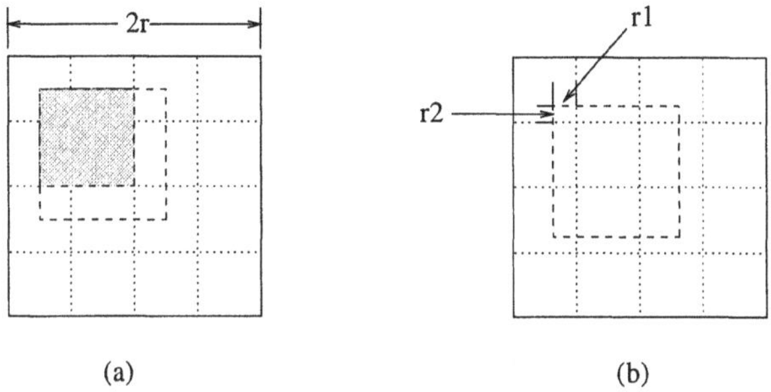

Figure 4. Covered area of query image by segments.

3. Texture-based Image Retrieval

In this section, we will investigate the application of the proposed image data model to content-based image retrieval in image database systems. A search procedure on the nona-tree is designed to compare the feature vectors between the query image and database images. Wavelet transforms will be used to generate the feature vectors of image segments.

3.1. Searching Nona-trees

Let database images be represented by their nona-trees. A procedure of feature generation is then applied to each node in the nona-tree. Thus, each node contains the feature vector of a segment rather than the original pixel data. Also, the feature vector is generated on the basis only of the pixel data of the node rather than the entire image.

We now consider an image database in which all images are represented by their feature vectors in nona-trees. Let Q be an query image. We discuss a procedure for matching the feature vector of the query image with that of the database images. A correspondence is first established between database image contents and feature vectors, and retrievals are then performed on the basis of the relationship between these feature vectors and the feature vectors of query image Q. We can then locate those images within a large image database which contain or are similar to the query image, as governed by set criteria.

A relationship between a given query image Q and any image $\mathcal{M}$ in the database is determined by comparing the feature vector of Q with different portions of $\mathcal{M}$. This can be done by traveling through the nona-tree of $\mathcal{M}$ from the root to the bottom. We use the root mean square metric to compare the distance between the feature vector of the query image and that of the image segments of the database images. That is, for given feature vectors $v_1(a_1, ..., a_n)$ and $v_2(b_1, ..., b_n)$, their distance is computed as follows:

$$dist(v_1, v_2) = \sqrt{\frac{\sum_{i=1}^{n}(a_i - b_i)^2}{n}} \tag{1}$$

For a given threshold t, if the distance between the query image and a segment of a database image is less than t, then we select this database image as a matched image.

Note that the above search of individual nona-trees may be highly time consuming. However, this problem can be circumvented by a novel indexing technique on the feature vectors generated from the image segments. Consider a feature space which contains all generated feature vectors of image segments. An indexing technique can be constructed to classify the feature vectors into different clusters based on their distances in the feature space [7]. For a given query image, an efficient retrieval can then be supported by search through the index. The details to construct an index on the feature space will not be discussed further in this paper.

3.2. Wavelet Transforms

A wide variety of wavelet-based image compression schemes have been reported in the literature. In this approach, compression is accomplished by applying a wavelet transform to decorrelate the image data, quantizing the resulting transform coefficients, and coding the quantized values. The central part of this process, wavelet transform, is what we want to examine. The data transformed by wavelets can be utilized for content-based retrieval.

Wavelet transform is a type of signal representation that can give the frequency content of the signal at a particular instant of time. Initially, regions of similar texture need to be separated out. This may be achieved by decomposing the image in the frequency domain into a full subband tree using filter banks [16]. In order to explore the advantage of deriving the texture features from compressed image format, the wavelet transform can be used for the subband decomposition [9]. Each of the subbands obtained after filtering has uniform texture information. Typical methods like energy estimation in subbands are used for feature extraction from the subbands.

Wavelet based subband coding allows simultaneously for high spatial resolution at high spatial frequencies and high spatial-frequency resolution at low spatial frequencies. Thus a filter bank based on wavelets could be used to decompose the image into low-pass and high-pass spatial-frequency bands [8].

Using a specific wavelet transform, feature extraction is performed on all image segments in the nona-trees. Three-level of subband decomposition is used [9]. Each of the subbands obtained after filtering have uniform texture information. In our experiments, the feature extraction was performed using Daubechies wavelet transform [14]. Each three-level transformation produces 10 subbands. The features were extracted by energy estimation in subbands. Two energy features, mean and variance, are computed on each subband. Thus, each feature vector has 20 elements. This feature extraction procedure is applied to all image segments in the tree representation of each image. Each node in the nona-tree thus represents a segment of the image and its feature vector.

3.3. *Experiments*

A testbed of the image database has been constructed from Brodatz texture images [3] and their variants. There are 112 different textures and 20 samples with each texture. The images are 96 × 96 pixels in size. The query images were chosen as random subimages of randomly chosen Brodatz images.

Given a query image, its feature vector is calculated using the above feature extraction approach. We then compare the distance between the query image and the image segments of the database images with a size greater than or equal to the size of the query image. Figure 5 presents four query images with the size 24 × 24 pixels, each of which is associated with the best selected four database images based on the distance comparison. The number under each database image in the figure indicates the distance between this database image and the given query image.

Let the position of each pixel in the image be represented by (x, y) coordinates, where x refers to the column position and y refers to the row position. Let $(0, 0)$ coordinates be at the most upper left point of the image. Table 3 presents the positions of the matched segments within the database images shown in Figure 5. For example, for query image Figure 5 (a), a matched segment was found in image d001p at the position of the 48th row and the 48th column with the size 24 × 24 pixels. This segment appear to be the subsegment 1 of segment 3 at the first depth nona-tree decomposition. Similarly, a matched segment was found in image d001j at the position of the 0th column and 24th row with the size 24 × 24 pixels. This segment appear to be the subsegment 3 of segment 1 at the first depth nona-tree decomposition. The exact positions of the matched segments are illustrated in Figure 5.

Table 3. Positions of matched image segments in database images

Test Image	matched segment position	size
d001p	(48,48)	24x24
d001j	(0,24)	24x24
d001d	(12,60)	24x24
d095p	(24,12)	24x24
d067m	(24,0)	24x24
d067d	(48,0)	24x24
d041j	(36,24)	24x24
d067i	(12,48)	24x24
d077o	(72,36)	24x24
d077s	(36,0)	24x24
d077n	(0,12)	24x24
d077t	(48,48)	24x24
d105k	(72,0)	24x24
d076t	(24,72)	24x24
d076o	(24,24)	24x24
d105l	(48,48)	24x24

Database images belonging to different texture groups but containing closely similar texture features may fall within a very small distance. As indicated in Figure 5, for example,

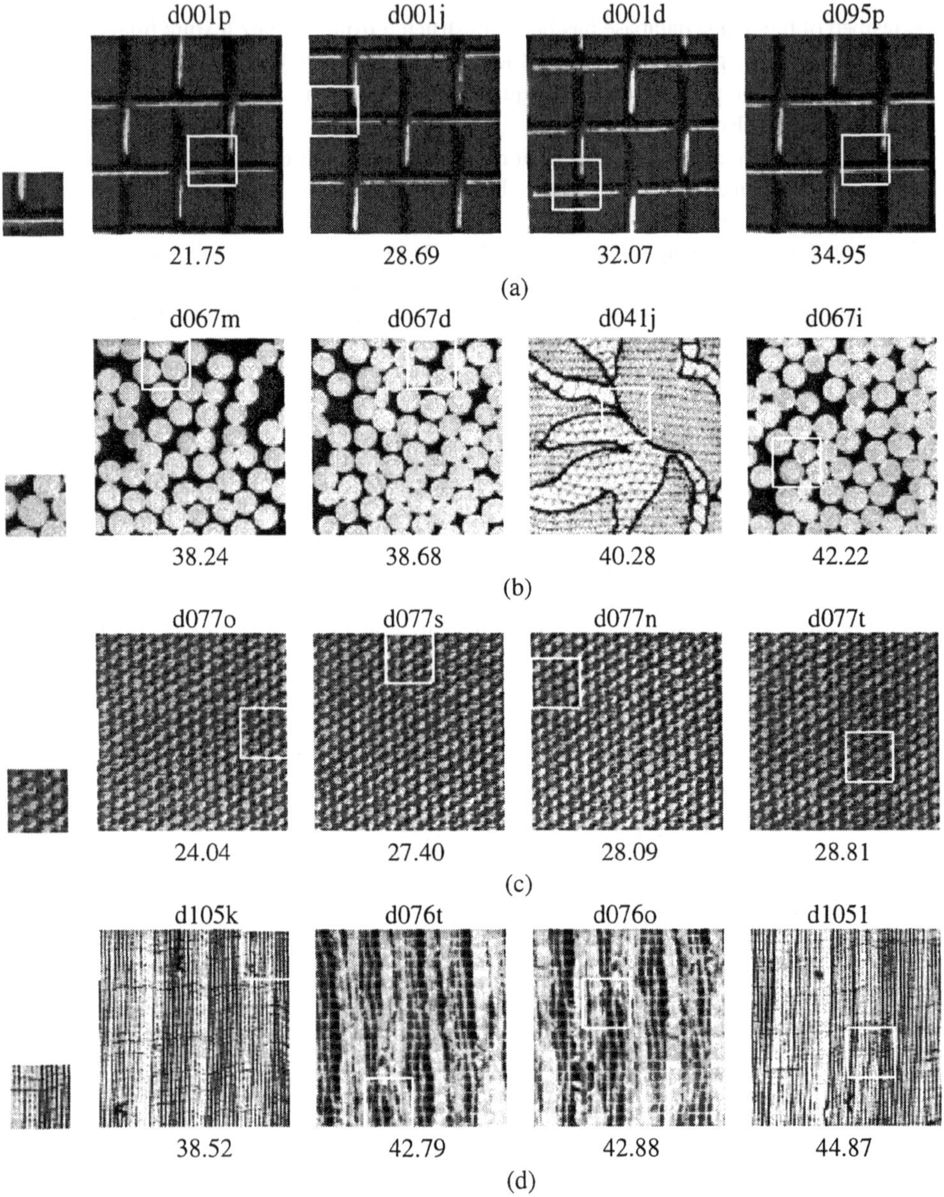

Figure 5. Iconic images and matched database images

d105k, d105l and d076t, d076o are in two different texture groups. However, the texture features in the two group contain closely similar texture features. A similar situation also occurs to the groups of d001 and d095.

Note that the selection of the threshold is application dependent. As shown in Figure 5, the minimum distance between similar images varies with different images. Also, note that some semantically irrelevant images may have feature vectors that fall within a very small distance. To prevent the retrieval of such irrelevant images, a clustering approach is needed to classify the images into different categories before retrieval is performed [20].

4. Discussions

In this section, we will discuss the retrieval effectiveness of the nona-tree decomposition using different wavelet transforms and compare the effectiveness of the nona-tree decomposition with other block-oriented decomposition approaches. We will also compare the block-oriented decomposition strategy with the traditional moving window analysis [13].

4.1. Retrieval Effectiveness with Different Wavelets

We now discuss the retrieval effectiveness of the nona-tree using different types of wavelet transforms. The retrieval effectiveness was calculated in terms of *recall* and *precision* [17]. Recall is defined as the ratio of the number of relevant images retrieved to that of the total relevant images in the database:

$$Recall = \frac{Retrieved\_relevant}{Total\_relevant}.$$

Precision is the ratio of the number of relevant images retrieved to that of all the images retrieved:

$$Precision = \frac{Retrieved\_relevant}{Total\_retrieved}.$$

The retrieval effectiveness for given query images varies on several aspects, including the locations of subimages in database images to which the query image is found to be similar, the size of query images and the types of wavelet transforms used to generate feature vectors.

In order to evaluate the retrieval effectiveness of various wavelet transforms, experiments were performed on two different types of wavelet transforms – Haar and Daubechies. Figure 6 presents the results of the retrieval experiments with these two wavelet transforms, while the query images are located close to the central areas of the upper, bottom, left, or right halves of the image segments of the database images. Based on these experiments, we see that the Daubechies with six coefficients is superior to the Daubechies with four coefficients and Haar in cases (a), (c), and (d). We also observe that Haar transform is superior to the Daubechies in case (b). Based on the experiments, the retrieval effectiveness of the nona-tree using wavelet transforms varies with application domains. Thus, the type of wavelet transform plays an important role in retrieval effectiveness. Experiments must be performed to determine which particular wavelet transform is best suited to any specific application domain.

In [19], we have introduced the nona-tree and its application in fractal-based image content retrieval. The nona-tree structure can also be used to search and match other image features, including color.

4.2. *Comparison with Other Block-Oriented Trees*

A quad-tree decomposition ensures that, if a portion of a decomposed image matches a query image, there then exists a segment which covers at least $\frac{1}{4}$ of the query image. Obviously, such a overlapping coverage may not be sufficient for supporting feature-based matching. Let us now consider a quin-tree which is similar to the nona-tree but omits segments 6, 7, 8, and 9 in each decomposition. A quin-tree decomposition ensures that, if a portion of a decomposed image matches a query image, there then exists a segment which covers at least $\frac{1}{2}$ of the query image.

We now compare the effectiveness of the quad-, quin- and nona-trees in content-based image retrieval. Our experiments are performed by selecting various subimages in the database images, which are remote to the central area of the database images, to be the query images. Retrieval based on these query images is then performed. Figure 7 presents the results of the retrieval experiments when a given query image is located at or very close to the central areas of the upper, bottom, left, or right halves of the image segment. In principle, the image segments in the nona-tree decomposition offer higher possibilities to match with such query images than those in the quad- and quin-tree decomposition. In experiments, we can see from Figure 7 that the query retrieval effectiveness using the nona-tree structure is much higher than using the quin- and quad-trees.

The query retrieval effectiveness using the quin-tree is also higher than using the quad-tree, especially when the query images are found to be similar to the subimages located in the central area of the database images. This illustrates that for query images which are located in such places in database images, the nona-tree decomposition offers a mechanism that is more effective in identifying relevant images. For those query images which are commonly covered by the image segments of quad-, quin-, and nona-trees, we observe that, in a recall range between 40 and 90 percent, the nona-tree structure offers the best retrieval precision results. For a recall range under 40 percent, nona-tree decomposition may not result in increased retrieval precision comparing with quad- or quin-tree decomposition, because a greater number of irrelevant images were identified by the nona-tree structure.

Moreover, we also observed that, when the recall is greater than 90 percent, the performance of all the trees degrades. However, the nona-tree structure is still performed better than both quin- and quad-tree structures. This can be attributed to the fact that, in case of the nona-tree, the query image is compared with more subsegments and there is a higher number of irrelevant images that get retrieved.

We now discuss the issue of whether the nona-tree structure should be further expanded. Theoretically, the block-oriented image decomposition can continue to expand the nona-tree structure to include more segments. Clearly, such a expansion will result in that, if a portion of a decomposed image matches a query image, there then exists a segment

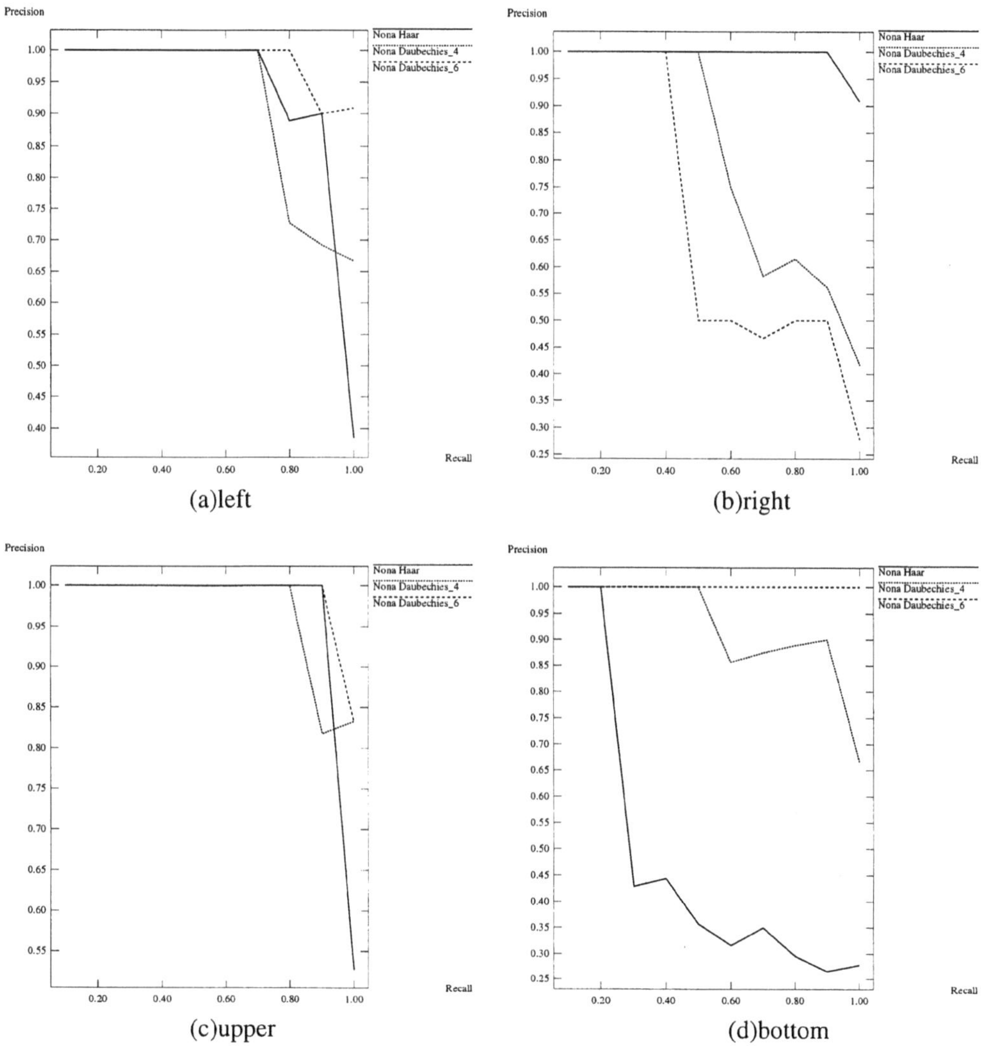

Figure 6. Retrieval effectiveness of Haar and Daubechies wavelet transforms.

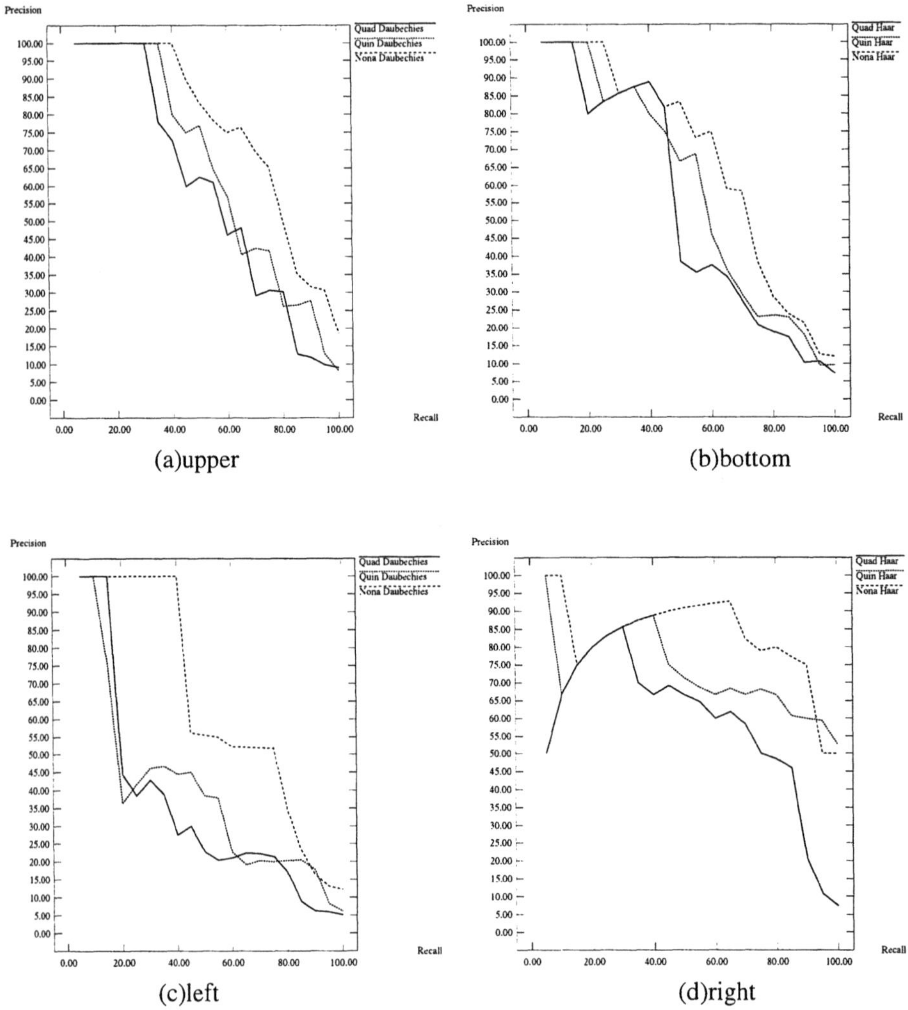

Figure 7. Retrieval effectiveness for a query image located at or very close to the central areas of the upper, bottom, left, and right halves of the image block.

in the decomposed image which covers more than $\frac{9}{16}$ of the query image. However, to guarantee evenly distributed segment decomposition and equally coverage of query images, the segments to be added at each level of tree decomposition is highly explosive. For example, the smallest number of subsegments to be decomposed for each segment to expand the nona-tree structure is 25 (Let us term this tree structure the 25-tree). The smallest number of subsegments to be decomposed for each segment to further expand the 25-tree structure is 81. We see that such a expansion will cause the feature space to explosively grow and seriously affect retrieval efficiency.

Thus, the trade-off between image retrieval effectiveness and efficiency must be considered in choosing a specific block-based decomposition strategy. Our experimental results indicate that the nona-tree structure is more effective than both quad- and quin-tree structure for certain query images. In addition, although the nona-tree structure increases the number of segments than the quad- or quin-tree structure, the retrieval efficiency can be remained by a good indexing technique.

4.3. Comparison with Traditional Moving Window Analysis

An alternative to hierarchical decomposition methods is the traditional moving window analysis. Here the signal processing argument is that the image, since it consists of projections of multiple objects, cannot be treated as a stationary stochastic process. Instead, it is reasonable to regard the image as having been generated by a short-space stationary process, where the signal (image) characteristics remain stable over a short-space and can change in adjacent spaces. The correct way to analyze such an image is by the use of an overlapping moving window. The size of the window is usually left unspecified as it is application dependent. However, there is a distinct relationship between the window size and overlap between windows, which can be derived based on sampling theory arguments. Specifically, it was shown in [12], that a minimum overlap of $N/2$ x $N/2$ for a moving window of size N x N must be maintained. From this observation, the quad-trees that do not maintain overlap between windows cannot do a complete analysis of the 2D short-space signal (image). By comparison, the nona-trees meet the minimum overlap requirement by having the segments at each level start at an offset of $N/2$.

For recognizing query objects in unsegmented images, the overlapping window method was used in [13]. There, a relation was derived between the window size (M_1, M_2), the shift in window (L_1, L_2) and the size of the query pattern (N_1, N_2) to be detected as:

$$M_1 + L_1 <= N_1 \tag{2}$$

$$M_2 + L_2 <= N_2 \tag{3}$$

If the moving window analysis was done using the above constraints, then it was shown that one of these windows was guaranteed to contain only the query pattern (if not all of it). With this tradeoff, we could design windows that captured any specified percent of query area by suitably varying M_i and L_i. It was also shown that a window containing only the query pattern can be detected even under pose changes by bounding the maximum pose change.

The disadvantage with this scheme is that it is very model-based in that, for each query, a different moving window analysis is required indicating that the windowing be done dynamically during querying rather than during database creation. One way to get around this is to categorize the queries in terms of size ranges and the moving window analysis per category can be done ahead of time. Alternatively, we can fix a window size for one-time moving window analysis (usually corresponding to the smallest query) and scale a given query region to the standard size before invoking search. But the disadvantage with these schemes is that to maintain the constraint described above, especially under pose changes, the windows may have to be very small, so that even if only the query region is isolated in the window, due to the small window size, the feature generation process may not give reliable features for matching to query region.

In contrast, the nona-tree decomposition can be considered as anticipating queries of different size and/or undergoing different pose changes for localization.

5. Conclusions

In this paper, we have conducted a study on image data representation and retrieval approaches to support effective and efficient retrieval of image data based on content. An effective block-oriented image decomposition structure, termed nona-tree, has been introduced to be used for content-based image retrieval. This decomposition structure offers a better block-oriented tree decomposition approach than the quad-tree decomposition. We have also discussed the application of the nona-tree data model to content-based image retrieval. Wavelet transforms were used to extract image features. Feature vectors of images were constructed using two wavelet transforms. Content-based image retrieval were performed by comparing the feature vectors of the query image and the segments in database images. Our experimental analysis have illustrated that the nona-tree decomposition offers a novel decomposition structure to be used to facilitate effective and efficient image retrieval.

References

1. M. Arya, W. Cody, C. Faloutsos, J. Richardson, and A. Toga, "QBISM: A Prototype 3-D Medical Image Database System," IEEE Data Engineering Bulletin, Vol. 16, pp. 38–42, 1993.
2. J.R. Bach, S. Paul, and R. Jain, "A Visual Information Management System for the Interactive Retrieval of Faces," IEEE Transactions on Knowledge and Data Engineering, Vol. 5, pp. 619–628, 1993.
3. P. Brodatz, Textures: A Photographic Album for Artists and Designers, Dover, New York, 1966.
4. S.K. Chang, Principles of Pictorial Information Systems Design, Prentice Hall, 1989.
5. S.K. Chang, C.W. Yan, Donald C. Dimitroff, and Timothy Arndt, An Intelligent Image Database System, IEEE Transaction on Software Engineering, Vol. 14, pp. 681–688, 1988.
6. T.-Y. Hou, P. Liu, A. Hsu, and M.-Y. Chiu, "Medical Image Retrieval by Spatial Features," in IEEE Conference on Systems, Man, and Cybernetics, 1992.
7. K.-I. Lin, H.V. Jagadish, and C. Faloutsos, "The TV-Tree: an Index Structure for High-Dimentional Data," The VLDB Journal, Vol. 3, pp. 517–542, 1994.
8. S. Mallat, "Multiresolution approximation and wavelet orthonormal bases of $l^2(r)$," Transactions of American Mathematical Society, Vol. 315, pp. 69–87, 1989.

9. S. Mallat, "A theory for multiresolution signal decomposition: the wavelet representation," IEEE Trnasactions on Pattern Analysis and Machine Intelligence, Vol. 11, pp. 674–693, 1989.
10. F. Rabitti and P. Savino, "Automatic Image Indexation and Retrieval," in Conference on Intelligent Text and Image Handling, 1991.
11. John R. Smith and Shih-Fu Chang, "Quad-Tree Segmentation for Texture-Based Image Query," in Proc. of ACM Multimedia 94, San Francisco, California, October 1994, pp. 279–286.
12. T.F. Syeda-Mahmood, "Attentional Selection in Object Recognition," PhD thesis, Department of Computer Science, MIT, May 1993.
13. T.F. Syeda-Mahmood, "Model-driven Selection Using Texture," in J. Illingworth, editor, Proceedings of the British Machine Conference, 1993, pp. 65–74.
14. G. Strang and T. Nguyen, Wavelets and Filter Banks, Wellesley-Cambridge Press, 1996.
15. A. Turtur, F. Prampolini, M. Fantini, R. Guarda, and M.A. Imperato, "IDB: An Image Database System," IBM Journal of Research and Development, Vol. 35, pp. 88–96, 1991.
16. P. P. Vaidyanathan, "Multirate Systems And Filter Banks," Prentice Hall Signal Processing Series, Prentice Hall, Englewood Cliffs, NJ, 1993.
17. C. J. van Rijsbergen, "Retrieval Effectiveness," in Karen Sparck Jones, editor, Information Retrieval Experiment, pp 32–43. Butterworths, 1981.
18. J. K. Wu and A. D. Narasimhalu, "Identifying Faces Using Mutiple Retrievals," IEEE Multimedia, Vol. 1, pp. 27–38, 1994.
19. A. Zhang, B. Cheng, and R. Acharya, "An Approach to Query-by-texture in Image Database Systems," in Proceedings of the SPIE Conference on Digital Image Storage and Archiving Systems, Philadelphia, October 1995, pp. 338–349.
20. A. Zhang, B. Cheng, and R. Acharya, "A Fractal-Based Clustering Approach in Large Visual Database Systems," The International Journal on Multimedia Tools and Applications, 1996, (to appear).

Edward Remias received his Bachelors in Electronics and Communication Engineering from the Regional Engineering College, Trichy, India. He is currently a graduate student in Electrical and Computer Engineering in the State University of New York at Buffalo. His research interests include image processing, content-based retrieval, and computer networks.

Gholamhosein Sheikholeslami is currently working towards the Ph.D. degree in Computer Science at the State University of New York at Buffalo. He received his BS (1989) in Computer Science from Tehran University, Tehran, Iran. He recieved an MS (1994) in Computer Science, and an MS (1995) in Electrical and Computer Engineering from the State University of New York at Buffalo. His research interests include multimedia database systems, content-based image retrieval, and image database clustering and indexing.

Aidong Zhang received her Ph.D. degree in Computer Science from Purdue University, West Lafayette, Indiana, in 1994. She is currently an Assistant Professor in the Department of Computer Science at the State University of New York at Buffalo. Her current research interests include transcation and workflow management, distributed database systems, multimedia database systems, educational digital libraries, and content-based image retrieval. She is a member of the IEEE Computer Society, ACM, and ACM SIGMOD.

Tanveer Syeda-Mahmood received her Ph.D. degree in Computer Science from the M.I.T AI Laboratories in 1993. She is currently a member of Research Staff at the Xerox Webster Research Center, Webster, New York, leading a program in image indexing of image databases. Her interests are in computer vision and image databases.

Multimedia Tools and Applications, 4, 171–197 (1997)

A Constraint-Driven Approach to Automate the Organization and Playout of Presentations in Multimedia Databases*

VELI HAKKOYMAZ veli@ces.cwru.edu
GÜLTEKIN ÖZSOYOĞLU tekin@ces.cwru.edu
Department of Computer Engineering and Science, Case Western Reserve University, Cleveland, OH 44106 USA

Abstract. We introduce a constraint-driven methodology for the automated assembly, organization and playout of presentations from multimedia databases. We use inclusion and exclusion constraints for extracting a semantically coherent set of multimedia segments. Presentation organization constraints are utilized for organizing the multimedia segments into a presentation, which in turn helps decide the playout order of the extracted multimedia segments. The playout order of the segments is represented in a presentation graph. If the specified set of organization constraints are not sufficient to construct a unique presentation graph, we propose two techniques so that a unique graph is constructible. We also propose two playout algorithms, one for the generation, start and termination of playout agents, the other for dynamic control of playout management on organized presentations. The characteristics of these algorithms are expressed in terms of presentation playout parameters.

Keywords: Multimedia Presentation, Presentation Organization, Playout Management, Playout Synchronization, Synchronized Presentation, Multimedia Databases

1. Introduction

In multimedia computing research, organizing various multimedia segments for a semantically coherent presentation, without any regard to the multimedia database that contains these segments, is an active research area under the title of *presentation managers*. Multimedia computing integrates different media types such as audio, video, text, and graphic images. Each medium can be modeled as a stream [13, 7, 6, 3, 19] which can be broken into a sequence of segments. A multimedia presentation refers to the presentation of multimedia segments using a number of output devices such as speakers for audio, monitors for text and video and so on. In this paper, we discuss the issues involved in automatically organizing presentations from multimedia databases. In particular, we introduce a methodology to automate the organization and playout of multimedia presentations.

The organization of presentations is a complex task in that the display order of presentation contents (in time and space) must be specified. Suppose that an education technologist is developing a presentation called *Training* that contains audio, video, and text media types. The critical decisions for presentation construction include (1) what the contents are, and (2) how the contents are organized (i.e., some parts of audio and video may be temporally related and have to be presented in parallel; some other parts can only be presented after certain subjects are covered, etc). Once the decision is made on the organization of the

* This research is partially supported by the National Science Foundation Grants IRI 92-24660 and IRI 96-31214

contents of the presentation, it must be conveyed to the end user in the correct organizational order and in a timely fashion.

In this research, we consider an environment where users request multimedia presentations of a fixed time length. For example, a user may request a one-hour long audio-video summary of a presentation about the programming language C^{++}. We also envision that the user (in some way) can specify the maximum number of monitor windows which can be open simultaneously for the presentation of parallel streams. Such a process can have multiple interactions between a user and the presentation system. For example, the system may respond to a user request by saying that the requested presentation cannot be performed in one hour if it is to be presented using the specified number of parallel windows. To automate the construction and playout of presentations, we propose a "constraint-driven approach". More specifically, we utilize

- *inclusion and exclusion constraints* for extracting a semantically coherent set of multimedia segments from the multimedia database,
- *presentation organization constraints* for organizing and deciding the playout order of the extracted multimedia segments,
- *playout-control constraints* in order to provide dynamic, playout-time controls for end users, and
- *physical-playout constraints* for helping to ensure a jitter- or hiccup-free playout of multimedia data.

We use inclusion and exclusion constraints between segments to facilitate the automated inclusion or exclusion of segments into a presentation. Consider an educational math lecture in video. In any presentation that contains a video sequence *Proof* illustrating the proof of a theorem, another video sequence *Thm* that defines the theorem should also be included. This is an *inclusion requirement* of *Thm* based on the included segment *Proof*. However, it is clear that *Thm* can be included in a presentation without including *Proof*. To summarize, when a user specifies (by pointing and clicking) a set of segments for a presentation, the $DBMS$, by using inclusion and exclusion constraints, adds segments into and/or deletes segments from the set in order to satisfy the inclusion and exclusion constraints. In a recent work[19] we have characterized inclusion and exclusion dependencies, axiomatized a subset, given two algorithms for automated presentation assembly, and discussed their complexity.

Presentation organization constraints allow the system to automate the organization of concurrent presentations of selected segments (that already satisfy inclusion and exclusion constraints). We assume that presentation organization constraints are entered into the database a priori by the database administrator, and, for any set of user-selected segments, the satisfaction of presentation organization constraints leads to an organized presentation. Consider the educational math video example. The video sequence *Proof* must be preceded (but not necessarily immediately) by another video sequence, say *Thm*, that defines the theorem. This is a *sequentializer constraint* for a presentation that contains *Thm* and *Proof* (as *Thm* should precede *Proof*). In this paper, we discuss how to organize a concurrent presentation (represented by a "presentation graph") by utilizing the presentation organization constraints. We assume that the database contains various presentation organization constraints. Users express a presentation organization query by specifying (a) an upper bound on the time length of the presentation, (b) an upper bound on the number of parallel monitor windows (for video playout) open at any time, (c) a set of selected segments (which are expanded, if necessary, into a set of "coherent" segments by utilizing inclusion and exclusion constraints and the algorithms of our earlier work [19]). Note that the requirement (b) specifies the maximum level of concurrency (i.e., the number of concurrently played-out video segments) at a given time. Since a computer monitor has a physical size limit, it (and, perhaps the computing power of the playout environment) has an upper bound on the number of concurrent segments (i.e., windows) it can effectively play. For example, clearly, playing out over 6 concurrent (monitor) windows at a given time is excessive. Such a requirement is captured by the requirement (b) above.

There is a tradeoff to satisfying requirements (a) and (b) at the same time, and we show in section 4 that this is an NP-hard problem. Therefore, rather than finding the optimum solution, we propose and evaluate two heuristics that allow us to obtain a unique presentation graph satisfying the requirements (a) and (b) in a near-optimum manner.

Once a concurrent presentation is specified (using the presentation graph), it needs to be played out [16, 10]. We associate a *playout agent* to each segment in the presentation, which is a lightweight process (a thread) that plays out the corresponding multimedia segment. In section 5.1, we describe a semaphore-based technique for the automated generation, synchronization and termination of playout agents in order to implement the concurrent presentation playout as defined by the presentation graph.

Another issue is to automate the incorporation of playout-time controls into the assembled presentation. Let A denote the action "Freeze all video streams that are currently being played out for 20 seconds". The presentation assembly system may designate a keyboard function key that, when pressed, sends the signal S which indicates to the "playout manager" software that the action A has to be taken. This is an example of the incorporation of event-action rules from active databases into the automated presentation organization problem. (One can extend this model to incorporate nonevents (negative events) and/or prohibited actions [14], as well.) When such rules, i.e., constraints, are incorporated into the automated presentation assembly problem, there is a tradeoff between their satisfaction and the satisfaction of other constraints. For example, when the above freeze occurs, the presentation time deadline may no longer be satisfiable, and a playout-time reorganization of the presentation graph may become necessary. We call such rule-based constraints *playout-control constraints*. In this paper, we discuss playout-control constraints with examples only.

presentation graph reorganization. For example, an action request such as the system reconfigures the presentation graph, checks for the declines depending on the satisfaction or unsatisfaction of length bound is of higher priority. However, an action request occurs first" is acceptable if it allows the satisfaction of the time length bound.

Issues such as physical playout constraints, hiccup-free playout, quality of service (QoS) guarantees and so on, which are closely related to media presentation, are not the focus of this paper. The approach we have taken in addressing these issues is described in [11].

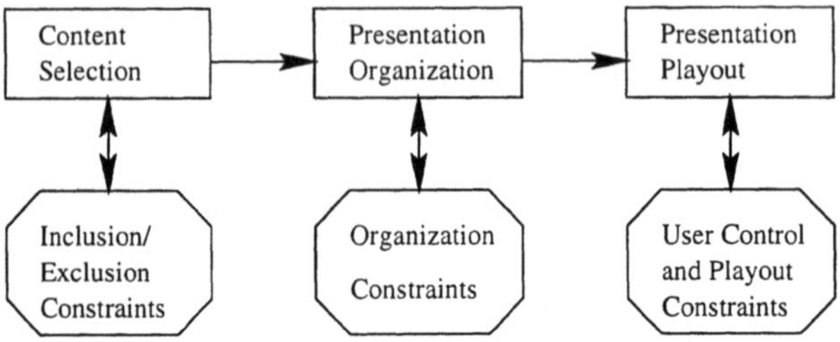

Figure 1. Multimedia Presentation System

Figure 1 shows the constraint types and their functionality in our multimedia presentation system. In the rest of this section, we briefly survey the related work on presentation and playout management issues. Section 2 presents the basic definitions used throughout this paper. Section 3 characterizes the organization constraints. In section 4, we formally define the presentation organization problem and discuss two heuristic methods as an approximation to its solution. In section 5, after organizing a presentation in section 4, we present two methods for the presentation playout. Section 6 gives the concluding remarks and the direction of future research.

1.1. Related Work

In recent years, attempts to tackle the problem of preparing multimedia segments into a multimedia presentation and conveyance of the resulting presentation for human users have gained momentum in the literature[15, 12, 5, 13, 16, 6, 19, 24, 20].

Little and Ghafoor in [16] made one of the earliest attempts to develop a temporal-interval based(TIB) model that captures the timing relationships among multimedia data segments. They assume that inter-segment temporal relations are either imposed at the creation time of the multimedia segments (i.e., called live synchronization) or set up artificially (i.e., called synthetic synchronization). In their work, presentation of each multimedia data segment is represented by a time interval (start time, end time, duration). Using this model with the timing information, they come up with a playout schedule for the segments with 'monotonically increasing deadlines' in order to present them in a timely manner. To this extent, they specify the temporal access algorithms to facilitate *forward* and *reverse playout* as well as *partial-interval evaluation* (for pause-resume operations).

The same problem is tackled by Hoepner [12, 13]. In these works, three distinct problems in multimedia presentations are identified as determining the contents as well as the layout of the presentation in time and space. However, the main focus of the work is concerned with the description of temporal aspects of an abstract presentation behavior. Synchronization and control of temporally related presentation actions are modeled by presentation frame types, *sequentializer, parallelizer, splitter, combiner, and brancher.*

These works mainly deal with modeling the way in which multimedia data segments are presented, but not the contents or the organization of multimedia presentations. As for the feasibility of providing presentations from multimedia databases over a distributed multimedia system, there have been several studies in describing the requirements and design of such systems[24, 20, 18].

Znati and Field in [24] focus on the design of the communication protocols, called ϕ-channel, to support guaranteed real-time communication for distributed multimedia systems. The ϕ-channel is a network level abstraction of a fractional, simplex, end-to-end communication channel between a source and a destination to support the requirements of real-time applications.

Another work in [20] by Qazi, Woo and Ghafoor states the need for a specification model for the communication and synchronization of multimedia segments in a distributed environment in order to realize successful retrieval, composition and presentation of multimedia segments.

2. Preliminary Definitions

We first identify the basic presentation organization constraints that enable users to express the flow of a multimedia presentation in terms of how and what order the segments are played out to the user, be it sequential, concurrent, or some combination of both. In this simple model, no time is involved in expressing the organization of multimedia segments. An expert user or presentation generator can express the presentation flow by specifying the presentation organization constraints for the multimedia segments that are contained in the presentation.

Basically, some segments may have to be played out in a sequential manner (i.e., one is before the other). We represent such a constraint between two segments (i.e., say a and b) as **sequential**(a,b) in the textual form and call it a **sequentializer** constraint.

Endings of the playout of some segments may signal the presentation to split into two or more streams, starting with a segment from each stream. Such a constraint involves at least three segments, one of which is considered to be a *designated segment*. After presenting the designated segment, the remaining segments are presented in parallel. We represent such a constraint among three segments (i.e., say a, b and c) as **split**(a, b, c) in the textual form, specify the first argument a as the designated segment, and call the constraint a **splitter** constraint.

The last presentation organization constraint type is the **merger** constraint, which indicates that, after two or more segments are presented in parallel (i.e., concurrently), they will merge into one stream, from which a designated segment will be presented. Like the splitter constraint, the merger constraint involves at least three segments, one of which is the designated segment. We represent such a constraint among three segments (i.e., say a, b, and c) as **merge**(a, b, c) in the textual form and specify the last argument c as the designated segment.

Note that no synchronization points (i.e., time values) are specified in this model. Only relative playout timings of segments are known.

A **presentation graph** $G = (V, E)$ is a directed graph which is augmented by two special nodes, *initial node* I and the *final node* F, where nodes in $V(G)$ are labeled with the segments in the presentation, and edges in $E(G)$ indicate the relative presentation order of two segments (i.e., $a \longrightarrow b$ specifies that segment a is "before" segment b in the presentation). Edges are added to a presentation graph according to the specified organization constraints. Figure 2(i) depicts a one-to-one correspondence between organization constraints in textual form and the corresponding graph components.

2.1. *Obtaining Subpresentations*

A subpresentation corresponds to a connected graph and we informally use the term **subpresentation** to refer to a structure that contains a collection of segments and organization constraints from which a presentation graph is constructible. A more descriptive definition will be given shortly.

Let $SS = (s_1, s_2, \cdots, s_n)$ denote the selected set of multimedia segments that are to appear in the presentation. Let $OC = (o_1, o_2, \cdots, o_t)$ denote the presentation organization constraints that are specified for SS.

Given any sets SS and OC, the subpresentations are constructed in two stages. In the first stage, the organizationally related segments are grouped together, and in the second, after augmenting with two extra nodes and a number of edges, each group becomes a subpresentation.

Stage 1: Grouping the Segments

1. Create a group C_i for each segment $s_i \in SS$.
2. Consider each organization constraint $o_i \in OC$ (in some arbitrary order).
   (A) If o_i is of type *sequential*(s_j, s_k)
      i. Let C_1 be the group that segment s_j belongs to, and let C_2 be the group that segment s_k belongs to.
      ii. Create a new group C_3 such that $C_3 = C_1 \cup C_2$.
      iii. Eliminate the groups C_1 and C_2 from further consideration.
   (B) If o_i is of type *split(a, S)* or *merge(S, a)* where $|S| = n \geq 2$,
      i. Let C_{n+1} be the group that a belongs to, and let $C_1, C_2, \cdots, C_n$ be the n groups that n segments in S respectively belong to.
      ii. Create a new group C_{n+2} such that $C_{n+2} = C_1 \cup C_2 \cup \cdots \cup C_n \cup C_{n+1}$.
      iii. Eliminate the groups $C_1, C_2, \cdots C_{n+1}$ from further consideration.

Let us assume that, after the segments are grouped, we end up with m groups, which we arbitrarily name as C_1, C_2, $\cdots$, C_m by changing the indices.

Stage 2: Augmenting the Groups into Subpresentations

Consider each group C_i, and create a graph G_i with the following nodes and edges $(1 \leq i \leq m)$:

1. Make a node for each segment in C_i and label it with the segment name.

2. For each organization constraint (as shown in Figure 2(i)) involving the segments in group C_i,

   (A) if it is of type *sequential(a, b)* where $a, b \in C_i$, add a directed edge from node a to node b (i.e., $a \longrightarrow b$) into the graph G_i.

   (B) if it is of type *split(a, S)* where $a \in C_i$ and $S \subseteq C_i$, add directed edges from node a to node s_i for each segment $s_i \in S$ (i.e., $a \longrightarrow s_i$) into the graph G_i.

   (C) if it is of type *merge(S, a)* where $a \in C_i$ and $S \subseteq C_i$, add directed edges from node s_i to node a for each $s_i \in S$ (i.e., $s_i \longrightarrow a$) into the graph G_i.

3. Determine the number of incoming and outgoing edges (i.e., $incoming\_edge\_count$ and $outgoing\_edge\_count$, respectively) for each node (i.e., segment) in G_i.

4. Create two additional nodes, the initial node I and the final node F.

5. For all nodes $v \in G_i$,

   (A) if $incoming\_edge\_count[v] = 0$ then add a directed edge from *the initial node I* to node v (i.e., $I \longrightarrow v$) into the graph G_i.

   (B) if $outgoing\_edge\_count[v] = 0$ then add a directed edge from node v to the *final node F* (i.e., $v \longrightarrow F$) into the graph G_i.

6. Add the additional nodes I and F into G_i.

Nodes I and F represent the start and terminate nodes, respectively, for each subpresentation. They both are empty (null) segments. After the augmentation, we call each graph G_i a *subpresentation*.

Example: Using the above procedure, we form a unique subpresentation graph from a given set of segments and organization constraints. Figure 2(ii) and (iii) depict the way the construction algorithm works. □

A multimedia presentation can be described as a particular arrangement of a collection of subpresentations. Each subpresentation G_i has a *source* (i.e., the segment that is to be presented first which is I in our case) and a *sink* (i.e., the segment that is to be presented last which is F in our case). Every node in a subpresentation is related to every other node through some specific temporal relation. Each subpresentation has a *length* (i.e., the maximum of the sums of the lengths of all segments on each path from the source to its sink) as well as a *height* (i.e., the maximum cut[17]) that is computed in a way that will be described shortly. We will also use the notion of *height at a point* for a subpresentation. Note that I and F nodes are introduced in each subpresentation. To provide unique node labels for a presentation graph constructed out of several subpresentations, we may easily rename I and F nodes of each subpresentation with unique labels (i.e., new indices). Yet these are the empty (null) nodes in the presentation graph. Thus, each presentation graph

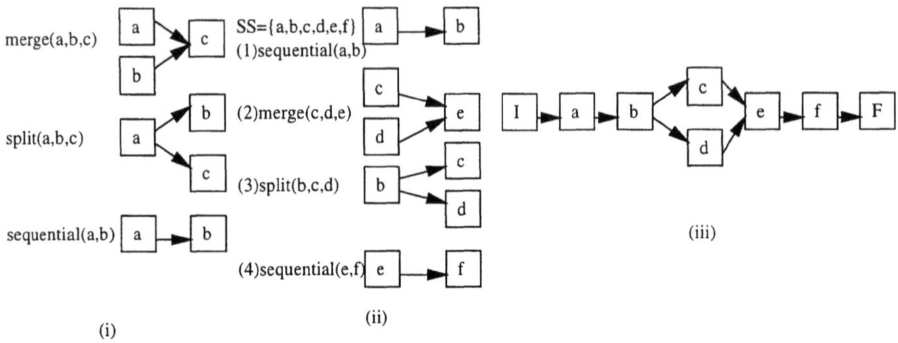

Figure 2. Relationship between Organization Constraints and Presentation Graph. (i) Simple organization constraints and their transformations into graph components, (ii) a set of constraints and the corresponding graph components, (iii) resulting presentation graph.

can be made to have only one unique I (initial) node and one unique F (final) node by introducing new indices.

Let G_i denote such a subpresentation for a presentation consisting of n subpresentations, $1 \leq i \leq n$. A particular arrangement for a collection of subpresentations means that all G_i's are merged into a single connected (presentation) graph G in such a way that (1) the user-specified limit on the presentation length is not exceeded, (2) the height of the resulting presentation is no more than a user-specified height limit. As an illustration, the maximum number of video segments that are presented in parallel must not exceed the available number of monitor windows for video (specified by the user). We use the term *height* to refer to the available number of monitor windows for video. In other words, "joining" a set of G_i's into a single directed graph means identifying the presentation organization constraints among all the G_i's.

3. Presentation Organization

In this section we characterize presentation organization constraints and discuss the presentation organization issues.

3.1. Presentation Organization Constraints

The purpose of presentation organization constraints is to automate the organization of a concurrent presentation containing the selected set SS of multimedia segments (which already satisfy presentation inclusion and exclusion constraints). We assume that presentation organization constraints are entered into the database a priori by the database administrator.

To summarize, we use the following presentation organization constraints:

Sequentializer (SQ) constraint between segments a and b: In any presentation with a and b, presentation of a is succeeded by the presentation of b.

Splitter (SP) constraint between segment a and segment set S: When a and any subset S' of S is in a presentation, the presentation of a is succeeded by a concurrent presentation of all the segments of S'.
Merger (MG) constraint between segment a and segment set S: When a and any subset S' of S are in a presentation, after all segments in S' are concurrently presented, they are merged into a single stream, and a is presented.

3.2. *Interpreting Presentation Organization Constraints*

Sequential(a, b) is equivalent to "*a meets b*" [1] where a and b represent two time intervals, and their relationship is that the interval b starts at the point where interval a ends. Assuming that S is a nonempty set of segments, two other organization constraints can be interpreted as follows: *Split(a, S)* is equivalent to *a meets s_i* $\forall s_i \in S$. However, consider the merger constraint *merge(S, a)*. In one case, segment a can start right after at least one of its immediate predecessors ends (i.e., *at-least-one semantics*). We can, therefore, set the starting time of the segment a as the ending time of the earliest ending predecessor segment. In another case, segment a can start only after all of its immediate predecessors end (i.e., *all semantics*). For this semantics, we have to set the starting time of the segment a as the maximum of the ending times of all the segments that immediately precede the segment a.

For the merger constraint, we can express these two semantics as follows: Let a be a segment, ST be the segment start time, and l be the playout duration of the segment. Then, for all segments p, where p is an immediate predecessor of segment a,

All Semantics:

$$ST(a) = \begin{cases} 0 & \text{if } a \text{ is a source node} \\ max\{ST(p) + l(p)\} & \text{otherwise} \end{cases} \tag{1}$$

At-least-one Semantics:

$$ST(a) = \begin{cases} 0 & \text{if } a \text{ is a source node} \\ min\{ST(p) + l(p)\} & \text{otherwise} \end{cases} \tag{2}$$

Example: Using the two semantics defined in equations (1) and (2), we can compute the start times (ST) of segments in the presentation graph as shown in Figure 3(i). The playout duration l of each node's segment is indicated in the lower-right corner of the corresponding node.

Using the all semantics, i.e., the equation (1), the upper graph in Figure 3(ii) shows the presentation graph of Figure 3(i) with the computed start times for the playout of each segment. The lower part of Figure 3(ii) shows the playout times of segments using a timeline diagram.

Using the at-least-one semantics, i.e., the equation (2), the upper graph in Figure 3(iii) shows the presentation graph of Figure 3(i) with the computed start times for the playout of each segment. The lower diagram of Figure 3(iii) shows the playout times of segments using a timeline diagram. □

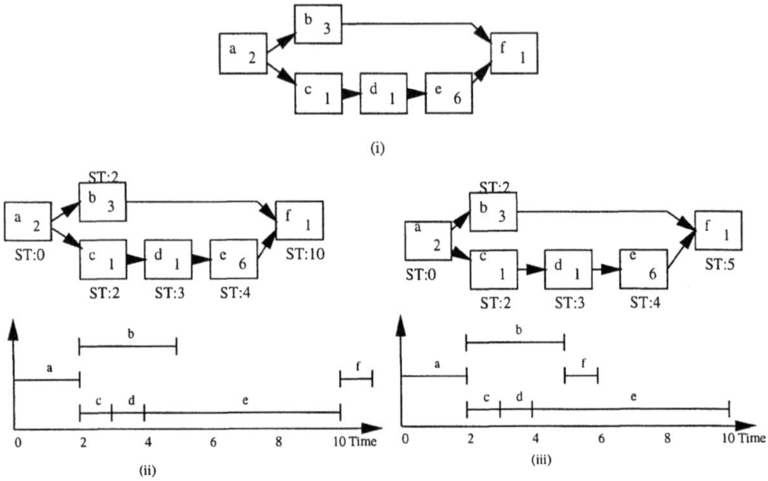

Figure 3. Computation of segment start times(ST) using two semantics of organization constraints. (i) a presentation graph, (ii) The same presentation graph with the ST of segments computed using the all semantics, (iii)The same presentation graph with the ST of segments computed using the at-least-one semantics

Note that there exists an anomaly for at-least-one semantics in the timeline diagram of Figure 3(iii): Even though the node f is designated as the final node in the presentation graph, it ends much earlier than one of its predecessors, namely, the segment e. Because of this anomaly, we use the all-semantics for the merger constraint in our examples in the rest of the paper.

3.3. *Controlling the Length and Height of a Presentation*

We call the set OC of presentation organization constraints a **cover** if a unique presentation is obtained by enforcing the constraints in the set OC. Assume that a set of presentation organization constraints is a *cover* for a given collection of multimedia segments. In this case, the task of forming a presentation is straightforward. After forming a presentation graph as described earlier, we use it to find the longest path from the initial node I to the final node F. The longest path gives us the length of the presentation. To satisfy the user-specified presentation length limit, the only thing that needs to be done is to check whether or not the user-specified length exceeds the computed presentation length.

As for the height computation, a simple algorithm that is presented in the next subsection can be used on the presentation graph. This algorithm finds the number of streams that need to be presented in parallel. As the number of parallel streams played out vary with time, we are only interested in the maximum number. By applying the algorithm between the start and end points of the presentation, we obtain a set of numbers, the maximum of which gives us the height of the presentation (i.e., the maximum number of monitor windows required to play out this presentation). We then check whether or not the user-specified height exceeds the computed presentation height.

However, the assumption of having presentation organization constraints forming a cover, and thus, leading to a unique presentation graph usually does not hold for real-world applications. In this case, there is at least one segment a that can be played out in parallel or sequentially with some other segment c without violating any presentation organization constraint in the set.

Assume that a certain segment c is at a fixed position in the presentation while another segment a is not. Segment a can be temporally placed anywhere with respect to c conforming to one of the possible cases as long as the length and height limits are not violated. If the placement of a causes no increase in the presentation length or height, then there is no need for length or height control. However, in the case of presentation length or height increase, we need to check whether or not the increase is tolerable. In other words, we need to make sure that the overall presentation length and height don't exceed the user-specified length and height limits, respectively. If the increase violates either the length or height limits, then we must find another temporal placement for the segment a where length and height limits are not violated.

3.4. Computing the Height of a Presentation

Given a subpresentation with a presentation graph, what is the maximum number of parallel windows needed for playing the video segments in the subpresentation? This problem is identical to finding the maximum "cut" in a given temporally-aligned graph. Therefore, the maximum cut corresponds to the height of the presentation. We give the following simple algorithm for this purpose.

Call the start and the end of each segment in a subpresentation as the *start* and the *end event* or simply *"event"*. Assuming that there are n segments in a subpresentation, the total number of events is $2n$. Events occur at specific time points which are called *event points*. The total number of event points can be fewer than the total number of events since multiple events may occur at the same event point. Therefore, the total number of event points is at most $2n$.

Since event points are time values (i.e., positive numbers), they can be ordered in increasing/decreasing order. Let m denote the total number of event points, where $m \leq 2n$, and *Event i* denote the group of events that occur at the ith event point, $1 \leq i \leq m$.

Height at a point, height of a subpresentation at any point in time (i.e., say, at time d) equals the height between event points for $Event\ j$ and $Event\ j+1$ where (1) event point for $Event\ j \leq d$, and (2) there does not exist an $Event\ i$ such that event point for $Event\ j$ $<$ event point for $Event\ i \leq d$, and (3) $j < m$. This is true because no new edge appears in the presentation graph between two consecutive event points.

Formally, an $Event$ will be characterized by $[E, S, T]$ where E is the event point (i.e., a positive number), S is the set of segments that start at E, T is the set of segments that end at E. After ordering the events in increasing order of event points, we denote each event with an index $[E, S, T]_i$ for the ith event, $i \leq m$, or an element of an event i as E_i, S_i, or

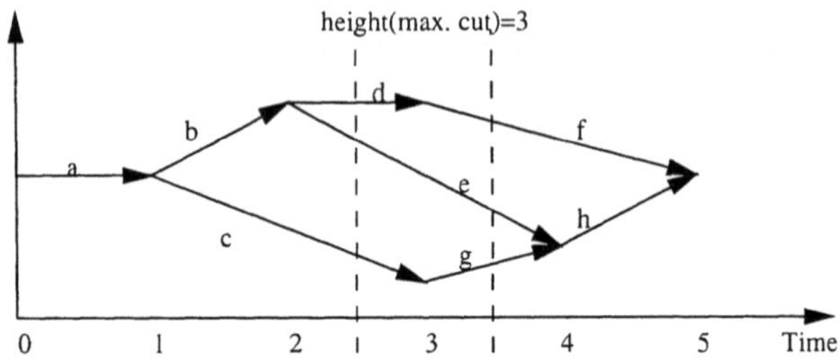

Figure 4. A Timeline Diagram Showing the Event Points of a Subpresentation Graph

T_i. For a subpresentation graph, since all the segments that start will eventually end, the following holds:

$$\sum_{i=1}^{m} | S_i | = \sum_{i=1}^{m} | T_i | \tag{3}$$

The height between any two consecutive event points (E_k and E_{k+1}, $k < m$) for a subpresentation is expressed by :

$$\sum_{i=1}^{k} | S_i | - \sum_{i=1}^{k} | T_i | \tag{4}$$

Example: Figure 4 depicts the segment playout behavior using a timeline diagram for a subpresentation graph. Using the notations introduced so far, the following events characterize this subpresentation (n=8; m=6):

$Event\ 1:$ [0, {a}, {}]
$Event\ 2:$ [1, {b,c}, {a}]
$Event\ 3:$ [2, {d,e}, {b}]
$Event\ 4:$ [3, {g,f}, {c,d}]
$Event\ 5:$ [4, {h}, {g,e}]
$Event\ 6:$ [5, {}, {h,f}]

Using the expression (4), the heights between two consecutive event points for this subpresentation graph are computed as follows:

height at $[0, 1) = 1 - 0 = 1$;
height at $[1, 2) = 3 - 1 = 2$;
height at $[2, 3) = 5 - 2 = 3$;
height at $[3, 4) = 7 - 4 = 3$;
height at $[4, 5) = 8 - 6 = 2$;
height at $[5, \infty) = 8 - 8 = 0$;

Thus, the height of this subpresentation is 3. □

4. Problem Definition

Recall that the subpresentations are $G_1, G_2, \cdots, G_n$.

First, let us define what we mean by the term **arrangement**: An arrangement of subpresentations means that each subpresentation G_j is connected to some other subpresentation(s) G_i and G_k without forming a cyclic graph in such a way that (1) the source node of G_j is an immediate successor of the sink node of G_i or the initial node I, (2) the sink node of

G_j is an immediate predecessor of the source node of G_k or the final node F. Recall that I and F nodes in subpresentations can be renamed (with new indices) so that nodes in the resulting presentation graph has unique labels.

Definition. Presentation Organization Problem (POP):
Instance: Given (1) a set P of n subpresentations $(G_1, G_2, \cdots, G_n)$ each of which with a height and a length denoted by $h(G_i)$ and $l(G_i)$ for $1 \leq i \leq n$, respectively, (2) a positive number, $Length \geq 0$, and (3) a positive integer, $Height \geq 0$,
Question: Does there exist an arrangement M for P such that (1) $length(M) \leq Length$, and (2) $height(M) \leq Height$?

We will consider a simplified version of the POP problem, called S_POP, where all the subpresentations are of equal length (i.e., $l(G_i) = c, \forall G_i \in P$ and c is a constant). To determine the complexity of S_POP problem, we consider a known NP-complete problem, namely, *Bin Packing* and find a polynomial time reduction from *Bin Packing* to *S_POP*.

Definition. Bin Packing Problem:
Instance: Given (1) a finite set U of items, a size $s(u) \in Z^+$ for each $u \in U$, (2) a positive integer bin capacity B, and (3) a positive integer K,
Question: Is there a partition of U into disjoint sets $U_1, U_2, \cdots, U_K$ such that the sum of the sizes of the items in each U_i is B or less?

THEOREM 1 S_POP *is NP-hard.*

Proof: We give the following transformation (reduction) from Bin Packing to S_POP:

The set U of items in Bin Packing is the same as the set P of subpresentations in S_POP. Each item has a size $s(u), \forall u \in U$ in Bin Packing, while in S_POP each subpresentation has a height $h(G_i), \forall G_i \in P$. The bin capacity B of Bin Packing corresponds to the user-specified $Height$ in S_POP. The number of bins, K, transforms to the number of intervals, N, each of which has a length c. Overall, the total length of all the intervals is determined as cN, which is the user-specified $Length$ in S_POP.

Now the question in Bin Packing becomes as:

Is there a partition of P into disjoint intervals $I_1, I_2, \cdots, I_N$, *(each with a length* c, *thus the overall length* cN*) such that the sum of the heights of the subpresentations in each interval* I_i *is less than or equal to* $Height$*?*

A "yes" answer to Bin Packing requires a "yes" answer to S_POP, and a "no" answer to Bin Packing requires a "no" answer to S_POP. It is obvious that the given transformation is polynomial. ■

As a consequence of the theorem, we no longer focus on finding an optimal solution to the POP problem, but instead attempt to find a "good" heuristic solution. The methods used for designing such algorithms tend to be problem specific [4, 8]. Two heuristics based on a combination of empirical studies and common-sense arguments are given next.

4.1. *Heuristic 1 : Maximum Parallelism*

This heuristic attempts to find the shortest-length presentation that satisfies all the organization constraints, the user-specified limits on the presentation length and presentation height. Note that subpresentations are constructed in order to satisfy the given set of presentation organization constraints.

The length of a presentation is at least the maximum of the lengths of its subpresentations because, in one extreme case, all the subpresentations will be played out in parallel and the subpresentation with the maximum length will determine the length of the presentation. However, a parallel playout of all the subpresentations may violate the user-specified height limit. Therefore, some of the subpresentations may need to be organized back-to-back (i.e., sequential). Heuristic1 first sets the presentation height with the user-specified *UHeight* and then tries to form a presentation with the minimum possible length still satisfying the POP problem. To do so, a subset of subpresentations are selected and linked together without exceeding the user-specified height and length limits. If all the subpresentations are linked together without exceeding the length limit, then the algorithm finds a presentation and declares "success". However, if there are subpresentations which are not linked yet, and the length limit *ULength* is not exceeded by the current length, then the length is incremented by a certain amount and the same process is repeated. In case the length is incremented above a threshold value, *ULength*, then the algorithm cannot find a presentation and declares "failure". The pseudo code of the Heuristic1 is shown below:

```
Algorithm Heuristic1(UHeight, ULength, P):
Input:
        UHeight, ULength: User-specified Height and Length bounds
        P: set of subpresentations $G_1, G_2, \cdots, G_n$
        each of which is given with height $h(G_i)$ and length $l(G_i)$
Output:
        success/failure in forming a presentation
Body:
        X := Policy1;
        TLength := 0;                                   /* tentative length */
        Remain := P;                                    /* set of unrelated Gi's */
        Pred :={I}; Presentation :={I};                 /* I: initial, F: final node */
        while Remain is nonempty do begin
            Choose (wrt X) a subset $R$ of Remain such that
                $\sum_{G_i \in R} h(G_i) \leq$ UHeight;
            TLength := TLength + max$\{l(G_i), \forall G_i \in R\}$;
            if TLength>ULength then begin
                TLength := 0; Remain := P;
                Pred := {I}; Presentation := {I};
                switch(X)
```

```
                    case Policy1: X := Policy2;
                    case Policy2: X := Policy3;
                    case Policy3: Exit with failure;
          end
          else begin
                    Remain := Remain - R;
                    Add R into Presentation by making every subpresentation in
                    Pred(ie, most recently added subpresentations) an immediate
                    predecessor of each subpresentation in R;
                    Pred := R;
          end
     endwhile
     Add {F} into Presentation by making it an immediate successor of every
     G_i in Pred;
     Return success with Presentation;
```

4.2. Heuristic 2 : Steady Flow

This heuristic attempts to find the lowest-height presentation that satisfies all the organization constraints, the user-specified limits on the presentation length and the presentation height.

The height of a presentation is at least the maximum of the heights of its subpresentations because, in one extreme case, all of the subpresentations will be played out sequentially and the subpresentation with the maximum height will determine the height of the presentation. However, a sequential playout of subpresentations may violate the user-specified length limit. Therefore, Heuristic2 first tries to form a presentation with the minimum possible height still satisfying the POP problem. To do so, it sets the tentative presentation height with the maximum of the heights of subpresentations. Afterwards, the subpresentations are selected and linked together incrementally without exceeding the user-specified height or length limits. If all the subpresentations are linked together without exceeding the length limit, then the algorithm succeeds in finding a presentation and declares "success". However, if the length limit is exceeded, then the tentative height is incremented by a certain amount, *delta*, and the same process is repeated, this time by allowing concurrent arrangements of subpresentations. In case the tentative height is incremented above a threshold value, *UHeight*, then the algorithm cannot find a presentation and declares "failure". Note that this heuristic allows the parallel arrangement of subpresentations. The pseudo code of Heuristic2 is given below:

```
Algorithm Heuristic2(UHeight, ULength, P, delta):
Input:
     delta: the amount of increment
```

```
        UHeight, ULength: User-Specified Height and Length bounds
        P: set of subpresentations G_1, G_2, ···, G_n, each of which is
        given with height h(G_i) and length l(G_i)
Output:
        success/failure in forming a presentation
Body:
        X := Policy1;
        THeight:=max{h(G_i), ∀G_i ∈ P}; TLength:=0; /* tentative height and length */
        Remain := P;                                        /* set of unrelated Gi's */
        Presentation :={I}; Pred :={I};                     /* I: initial, F: final node */
        while Remain is nonempty do begin
            Choose (wrt X) a subset R of Remain such that
                Σ_{G_i ∈ R} h(G_i) ≤ THeight;
            TLength := TLength + max{l(G_i), ∀G_i ∈ R}
            if (TLength > ULength) then
                if (THeight ≥ UHeight) then begin
                    THeight := max{h(G_i), ∀G_i ∈ P};
                    TLength := 0; Remain := P;
                    Pred := {I}; Presentation := {I};
                    switch(X)
                    case Policy1: X:= Policy2;
                    case Policy2: X:= Policy3;
                    case Policy3: Exit with failure;
                end
                else begin
                    THeight:= min{UHeight, THeight+delta};
                    TLength:= 0; Remain:= P;
                    Presentation:= {I}; Pred:= {I};
                end
            else begin
                Remain := Remain - R;
                Add R into Presentation by making every subpresentation in
                Pred(ie, most recently added subpresentations) an immediate
                predecessor of each subpresentation in R;
                Pred := R;
            end
        endwhile
```

Add {F} into Presentation by making it an immediate successor of every
G_i in Pred;
Return success with Presentation;

Note that at each iteration within the while loop of both algorithms, choosing a subset of subpresentations can be performed in many different ways. Currently, we have three policies:

- Policy1 : Choose the subpresentations with "small" heights, the summation of which must not exceed the prespecified height.

- Policy2 : First choose subpresentations with "large" heights, the summation of which must not exceed the prespecified height. Then choose subpresentations with "small" heights, where the total height is less than Uheight. It is possible that we can still fit more subpresentations with small heights into the presentation without exceeding the prespecified height. Therefore, in this policy, we add subpresentations with large heights first, and then subpresentations with small heights into the presentation.

- Policy3 : Choose subpresentations in random, the summation of whose heights must not exceed the prespecified height.

Both heuristics use policy1, policy2, and policy3 (in this order) to form a presentation. If a presentation which satisfies the length and height constraints is found, then the algorithm declares success and returns the presentation. Otherwise, after all three of the policies are exhausted, it gives up and declares failure.

4.3. Empirical Evaluation of Heuristic1 and Heuristic2

To better understand the working principles of two heuristics and to see the effects of the user-defined parameters on each of them, we have performed a number of tests by simulating these two algorithms. In our simulation environment, the selected set of segments for presentation are assumed to be grouped and augmented to 20 subpresentations according to the method described in section 2.1. Heights and lengths of subpresentations are obtained from a uniform distribution between (1..6) and (1..10), respectively. For each set of input parameters supplied by the user, we generate 1000 sets of these subpresentations and, for each set of subpresentations, try to form a presentation graph conforming to the user-specified height and length constraints.

In summary, the simulation input specifies (1) the desired presentation height, UHeight, (2) the desired presentation length, ULength, and (3) number N of subpresentations to organize (i.e., 20).

After these specifications are given, the simulation system performs the following a certain number of times: (i) a new seed value is determined for the random-number generator, (ii) using the random-number generator, N subpresentations are generated, (iii) the heights of the subpresentations are obtained from a uniform distribution in the range of (1..6), (iv) the lengths of the subpresentations are obtained from a uniform distribution in the range of (1..10), (v) subpresentations are ordered with respect to their heights.

Finally, the Algorithms Heuristic1 and Heuristic2 are applied using the generated subpresentations.

Figure 5(i) shows that for the relatively small values of UHeight and ULength, the heuristics cannot find any presentation satisfying the constraints. As their values grow, the number of times the heuristics successfully find a presentation increases. Heuristics always find a presentation when the height and length constraints are set to large values. The plot in Figure 5(ii) is drawn by setting UHeight to a value so that in each trial a presentation is found. The plot shows the average lengths of the presentations computed by two heuristics against the user-specified ULength. As expected, Heuristic1 always produces short presentations in length compared to the Heuristic2. Thick, straight diagonal line is the maximum length tolerable for the presentations. The other plot in Figure 5(iii) is drawn by setting ULength to a value so that in each trial a presentation is found. The plot shows the average heights of the presentations computed by two heuristics against the user-specified UHeight. As expected, Heuristic2 always produces short presentations in height compared to the Heuristic1. Thick, straight diagonal line is the maximum height tolerable for the presentations.

5. Presentation Playout

After assembling a presentation which satisfies all of the given presentation organization constraints, and user-specified length and height limits on the presentation height and length, we now discuss dynamic playout control issues in an automated multimedia presentation environment.

5.1. *Generation, Start, and Termination of Playout Agents*

In order to describe the design of generic policies for a multimedia playout system in terms of timing parameters (of a real-time system [2, 9, 21]), we first discuss our playout model and its characteristics.

We associate a *playout agent (PA)* to each segment to be presented. A PA is a schedulable entity (i.e., a lightweight process) within the operating system and responsible for playing out the associated segment. Segments are played out at appropriate times on specific types of output devices depending on the segment's media type. The following parameters describe the characteristics of a PA:

- *Arrival time* (denoted by a_i for segment i), at which the corresponding segment has been fetched from its source and brought to the presentation playout site.
- *Earliest start time* (denoted by r_i for segment i), the PA can start playing out the segment i anytime after r_i.
- *Actual start time* (denoted by p_i for segment i) at which the PA starts playing out the segment i.

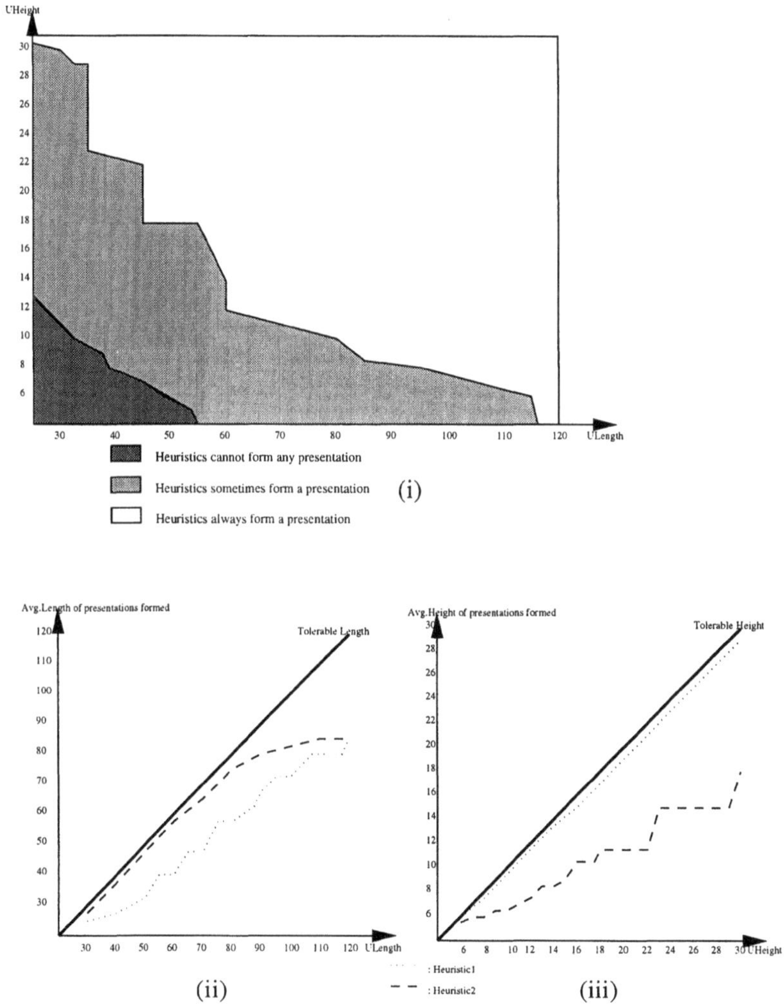

Figure 5. Evaluation of two heuristics. (i) Effects of user-specified height and length bounds on finding a presentation, (ii) User-specified length bounds vs. Average lengths of presentations constructed by two heuristics, (iii) User-specified height bounds vs. Average heights of presentations constructed by two heuristics.

Table 1. First Playout Algorithm.

1. Order the events in the presentation in increasing order of event points.
2. Consider each event (in order) with event point E_i
   (A) For each segment v in T_i,

   Terminate the PA for v;

   SignalSV(v_T);

   (B) For each segment u in S_i,

   SignalSV(u_{ST});

   Start the PA for u;

   (C) Wait until the next event point E_{i+1}.

- *Playout duration* (denoted by x_i for segment i), during which the PA continuously plays out the segment i.
- *Deadline* (denoted by d_i for segment i), by which the PA is expected to complete its playout of the segment.
- *Actual finish time* (denoted by f_i for segment i), at which the PA completes playing out the segment i.

A PA associated with any segment a has the following pseudo code:

```
WaitforSV(a_ST);
   Present segment a on its output device in time x_a;
SignalSV(a_T);
```

WaitforSV and SignalSV are binary semaphore primitives for synchronization purposes [18, 22, 23]. Concurrent activities typically require synchronization points so that slow activities can catch up faster ones, or fast activities are slowed down to let the other not-so-fast activities to come close and meet them at these points. Each synchronization point is represented as a synchronization variable or SV (i.e., a binary semaphore). Such a variable, if set, indicates that the synchronization point has been reached; otherwise, this point has not been reached. For each segment a, we create two unique SVs, one for the start (a_{ST}) and one for the terminate (a_T), both are unset, initially.

The following primitive operations are used on these variables: WaitforSV(SVExpr): to wait for the expression to become true. SignalSV(SV): to set the variable SV. SV is a single synchronization variable and SVExpr is an expression involving any number of SVs separated by the *and* operator. At the beginning, all SVs are unset. A presentation playout session starts with SignalSV(I_{ST}). Using the notation introduced in section 3.4, we give, in Table 1, our first playout algorithm. Note that in the algorithm if a PA completes its task in time less than its playtime duration, there is no early start for the consecutive PAs. They have to wait until the next event point. On the other hand, if a PA cannot complete its task in its playtime duration, it is terminated at the time point where the display of the segment is supposed to finish, and the consecutive PAs starts immediately. Using the parameters describing the characteristics of PAs, the properties of the first playout algorithm can be specified as in Table 2.

Table 2. Specification of first playout algorithm in terms of timing parameters.

Parm. setting	Meaning
$a_i = 0$;	All the segments are ready at the beginning at presentation playout site.
$p_i = r_i$;	All the PAs start playing out their segments at the earliest start time.
$d_i=r_i + x_i$;	All PAs must complete playing out their segments in x_i units of time.
$f_i = d_i$;	All the PAs complete playing out their segments at specified deadline.

Notice that the algorithm in Table 1 is static, meaning that the behavior is predetermined. However, due to media-related processing (for example, fetching, uncompressing or decoding very large video (MPEG) or audio files), or the heavy workload, CPU time is consumed. As a result, there will be delays in scheduling the PAs. The net effect is (1) information loss by skipping some frames, or (2) drop in frame rates, etc. To prevent such cases, we propose, in Table 3, a dynamic, on-line playout algorithm:

Example: Using the organization constraints (1) to (4) of the subpresentation graph shown in Figure 6, we can easily modify the PAs so that a complete synchronization of the playout activities is achieved.

Table 3. Second Playout Algorithm.

1. For each node v in the presentation graph, create two synchronization variables, one for start(v_{ST}) and one for terminate(v_T).
2. Generate a PA with the following (pseudo)code for each segment a:

   WaitforSV(a_{ST});

   Present segment a on its output device;

   SignalSV(a_T);
3. For each organization constraint (i.e, observed in the presentation graph),

   (A) if it is Sequential(a,b), add SignalSV(b_{ST}) at the end of PA for a.

   (B) if it is Split(a,b,c), add SignalSV(b_{ST}) and SignalSV(c_{ST}) (in this order) at the end of PA for a.

   (C) if it is Merge(b,c,d), add WaitforSV(b_T and c_T) and SignalSV(d_{ST}) (in this order) at the beginning of PA for d.

(1) Sequential(I,b)

(2) Split(b,c,d)

(3) Merge(c,d,e)

(4) Sequential(e,F)

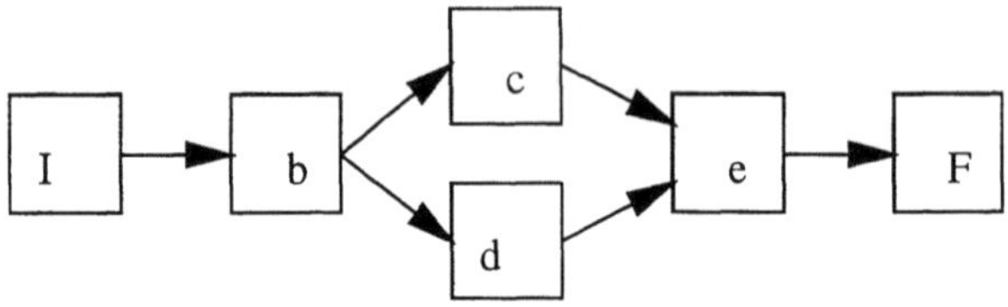

Figure 6. A Subpresentation Graph constructed out of constraints (1) to (4)

Table 4. Specification of second playout algorithm in terms of timing parameters.

Parm. setting	Meaning
$a_i = 0$	All the segments are ready at the beginning at presentation playout site.
$p_i = r_i \mp D_{i1}$	All PAs start playing out their segments in close range of their release times.
$d_i = r_i + x_i \pm D_{i2}$	All PAs can complete playing out their segments in the range of time x_i
$f_i = d_i \pm D_{i3}$	All PAs complete playing out their segments in the range of their deadlines.

PA for I:
WaitforSV(I_{ST});
present I;
SignalSV(I_T);
SignalSV(b_{ST});by (1)

PA for b:
WaitforSV(b_{ST});
present b;
SignalSV(b_T);
SignalSV(c_{ST});by (2)
SignalSV(d_{ST});by (2)

PA for c:
WaitforSV(c_{ST});
present c;
SignalSV(c_T);

PA for d:
WaitforSV(d_{ST});
present d;
SignalSV(d_T);

PA for e:
WaitforSV(c_T *and* d_T);by (3)
SignalSV(e_{ST});by (3)
WaitforSV(e_{ST});
present e;
SignalSV(e_T);
SignalSV(F_{ST});by (4)

PA for F:
WaitforSV(F_{ST});
present F;
SignalSV(F_T);

□

A presentation playout session starts with SignalSV(I_{ST}). In terms of characteristic timing parameters, this algorithm can be expressed as in Table 4.

By looking at the values of D_{i1}, D_{i2} and D_{i3}, one can study/observe the system characteristics in terms of where and how much delays/speedups occur in a presentation playout.

5.2. Execution-Time User Control During the Playout

To allow interactive user controls during the playout of an automatically generated presentation, an arbitrary number of (keyboard) buttons are reserved for the user interaction. Through these buttons, the user is able to change/affect the flow of the presentation in certain ways.

Example: The followings illustrate such a control mechanism:

1. Pressing the function key $F1$ and entering the value y has the effect that all streams are frozen for y seconds.
2. Pressing the function key $F2$ and entering the value y has the effect that the specified streams are frozen for y seconds.
3. Pressing the function key $F3$ and entering the value x has the effect that, for the rest of the presentation, the maximum number of concurrent windows must be equal to x.
4. Pressing the function key $F4$ and entering the value x has the effect that, for the rest of the presentation, the minimum number of concurrent windows must be equal to x.
5. Pressing the function key $F5$ and entering the value y and object id of the content-object o has the effect that any stream containing a representative frame with content-object o is frozen for y seconds.
6. Pressing the function key $F6$ has the effect that all streams that are currently being played out are frozen until the $ContinueButton$ is pressed.
7. Pressing the function key $F7$ and pointing and clicking a number of streams has the effect that the specified streams are frozen until the $ContinueButton$ is pressed.
8. Pressing the function key $F8$ and entering the object id of the content-object o has the effect that any stream containing a representative frame with the content-object o is frozen until the $ContinueButton$ is pressed.

□

All of these user controls can be modeled with the event-action paradigm of active databases[14, 21]. In general, $e \Longrightarrow A$ indicates that whenever the event e occurs, the action A must be taken. In all of the above examples, pressing a keyboard function key corresponds to an event, and its requested effect corresponds to the action taken by the presentation manager.

$Event_a$: Press function key $F1$ and enter value y.
$Action_a$: Freeze all streams for y seconds.
$Event_b$: Press the function key $F6$.
$Action_b$: Freeze all streams until the $ContinueButton$ is pressed.

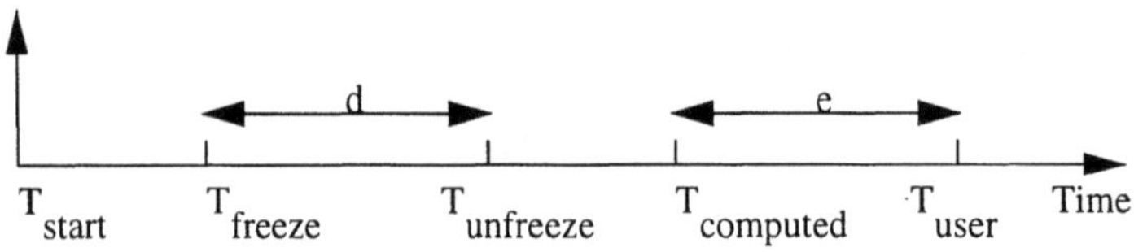

Figure 7. Significant time points during a presentation playout

The overall meaning of these two events and actions are the same for our model: upon the occurrence of either of these two events, the presentation pauses for d time units, where d equals either y or the time duration between the occurrence of the event and the pressing of the $ContinueButton$. Figure 7 shows the significant points on a timeline during a presentation playout. Significant points are described below:

T_{start} is the time point at which the playout of the presentation starts. T_{freeze} is the time point at which $Event_a$ or $Event_b$ occurs. $T_{unfreeze}$ is the time point at which the playout of the presentation resumes. $T_{computed}$ is the time point at which the playout of the presentation is supposed to end. T_{user} is the time point corresponding to the user-specified presentation length, ULength.

To analyze the incorporation of such event-action rules into our automated presentation organization model, we classify the segments of a multimedia presentation during a presentation playout into three groups: (i) Group D of segments that are already presented (i.e., Done), (ii) Group C of segments that are currently playing (i.e., Currently playing), (iii) Group Y of segments that are yet to play (i.e., Yet to play). For their incorporation, we create a new initial node I and make it an immediate predecessor of each segment in C (i.e. node that is labeled with the segment name) and the playout resumes with the newly added node I.

To determine whether we need a reorganization of the remaining portion of the presentation, we first compute the quantities d (i.e., $T_{unfreeze}$-T_{freeze}) and e (i.e., T_{user}-$T_{computed}$). Moreover, we find out the value of $rollback$=max$\{l(m_i), \forall m_i \in C\}$ where l is the playtime duration of the segment, since we may have to "rollback" the playout at most $rollback$ units to go back to the beginning of the segments that were playing at the time of the occurrence of the freeze event. The overall delay caused by this event is at most $d + rollback$. Therefore, if $d + rollback \leq e$, then no reorganization is needed. Otherwise, one has to do an incremental reorganization. This issue is currently being researched.

6. Conclusion and Future Work

In this paper, we have introduced a constraint-driven methodology for the automated assembly, organization and playout of presentations from multimedia databases. It is shown that the presentation organization problem is nontrivial. If the specified set of organization constraints are not sufficient to construct a unique presentation graph, we propose heuristic techniques so that a unique graph is constructible. After a presentation graph is constructed, we propose two playout management techniques, one for the generation, start and termination of playout agents, the other to provide dynamic (playout-time) controls for playout management. The playout characteristics are expressed in terms of presentation playout parameters.

We are currently implementing a prototype system to observe/understand the playout characteristics by experimenting with the timing parameters, which we intend to use in a multimedia presentation system. For the time being, a single host site is responsible for (1) the selection of presentation contents, (2) organizing the selected contents into a presentation, and (3) playing out the presentation to the user. As a future step, we plan to extend this work into a distributed environment, where the multimedia data (i.e., segments) and related constraints reside on a server site and the tasks related to selection and organization of contents into a presentation are carried out by local hosts (clients). The server is responsible for providing the clients with the available metadata (i.e., inclusion/exclusion constraints, set of multimedia segments, and organization constraints) of a particular subject in multimedia upon a client's request as well as feeding the clients with the contents of the presentation (i.e., the set of selected segments). We think that these extensions are easier due to the use of open system concepts[1] in most of our design decisions.

Acknowledgments

The first author is indebted to Prof. Taeib Znati at University of Pittsburgh for providing the encouragement and guidance for the development of this paper, as well as for reading the manuscript and making invaluable comments. He also would like to thank his fellow graduate students Erdogan Dogdu and Yanina Boguslavskaya, both at Case Western Reserve University, for discussing the subject and offering him their feedbacks. Lastly, he expresses his gratitude towards the anonymous reviewers.

Notes

1. *An open system* is the one that can be incrementally extended with the addition of new functionality without disturbing the existing system components.

References

1. J. F. Allen, "Maintaining knowledge about temporal intervals," Communications of the ACM, Vol. 26, pp. 832–843, 1983.
2. N. Audsley and A. Burns, "Real-time system scheduling," Technical Report YOR 134, University of York, Department of Computer Science, 1990.
3. D. Bordwell and K. Thompson, Film Art An Introduction, McGraw-Hill Inc., 4 edition, 1993.
4. Thomas H. Cormen, C.E. Leiserson, and R.L. Rivest, Introduction to Algorithms, The MIT Press, 1990.
5. Roger B. Dannenberg, Tom Neuendorffer, J. M. Newcomer, Dean Rubine, and David B. Anderson, "Tactus: toolkit-level support for synchronized interactive multimedia," Multimedia Systems, Vol. 1, pp. 77–86, 1993.
6. G. Davenport, T.A. Smith, and N. Pincever, "Cinematic primitives for multimedia," IEEE Computer Graphics & Applications, pp. 67–74, 1991.
7. D. Le Gall, "Mpeg: A video compression standard for multimedia applications," Communications of the ACM, Vol. 34, pp. 46–58, 1991.

8. M.R. Garey and D.S. Johnson, Computers and Intractability: A Guide to the Theory of NP-Completeness, W.H. Freeman and Company: New York, 1979.
9. Marc H. Graham, 11Issues in real-time data management," Real-Time Systems, Vol. 4, pp. 185–202, 1992.
10. V. Hakkoymaz and G. Ozsoyoglu, "Automating the organization of presentations for playout management in multimedia databases," in Proc. of the 1996 Int'l Workshop on Multi-Media Database Management Systems, Aug 1996.
11. Veli Hakkoymaz and G. Ozsoyoglu, "Automated assembly, organization and playout of multimedia presentations as a constraint-driven approach," Technical report, Case Western Reserve University, 1996, in preparation.
12. Petra Hoepner, "Presentation scheduling of multimedia objects and its impact on network and operating system support," in Network and Operating System Support for Digital Audio and Video, 1991.
13. Petra Hoepner, "Synchronizing the presentation of multimedia objects-oda extension," ACM SIGOIS Bulletin, Vol. 12, pp. 19–32, 1991.
14. Huang-Cheng Kuo and Gultekin Ozsoyoglu, "A framework for cooperative real-time transactions," in Proceedings of The First International Workshop on Real-Time Databases: Issues and Applications, March 1996.
15. T. D. C. Little, "A framework for synchronous delivery of time-dependent multimedia data," Multimedia Systems, Vol. 1, pp. 87–94, 1993.
16. T.D.C. Little and A. Ghafoor, "Interval-based conceptual models for time-dependent multimedia data," IEEE Trans. on Knowledge and Data Engineering, Vol. 5, 1993.
17. C. L. Liu, Introduction to Combinatorial Mathematics, McGraw-Hill, 1968.
18. C. Nicolaou, "An architecture for real-time multimedia communication systems," IEEE Journal on Selected Areas in Communications, Vol. 8, pp. 391–400, 1990.
19. G. Ozsoyoglu, V. Hakkoymaz, and J. Kraft, "Automating the assembly of presentations from multimedia databases," IEEE Int. Conf. on Data Engineering, February 1996.
20. N.U. Qazi, Miae Woo, and Arif Ghafoor, "A synchronization and communication model for distributed multimedia objects," ACM Multimedia, June 1993.
21. Krithi Ramamritham, "Real-time databases," International Journal of Distributed and Parallel Databases, 1992.
22. A. Silberschatz, J. Peterson, and P. Galvin, Operating System Concepts, Addison-Wesley Publishing Company, third edition, 1991.
23. Andrew S. Tanenbaum, Modern Operating Systems, Prentice Hall, 1992.
24. Taieb Znati and Brian Field, "A network level channel abstraction for multimedia communication in real-time networks," IEEE Transactions on Knowledge and Data Engineering, Vol. 5, pp. 590–599, 1993.

Veli Hakkoymaz was born in Adana, Turkey in 1964. He received the BS degree in computer science and engineering from Hacettepe University in Ankara, Turkey in 1987. He came to the USA in 1989 and earned the MS degree in computer science from University of Pittsburgh, Pittsburgh, PA in 1992.

Currently, he is a PhD student in Computer Engineering and Science Department of Case Western Reserve University in Cleveland, OH. His current research involves the presentation assembly and playout in multimedia databases.

Gültekin Özsoyoğlu received the BS degree in electrical engineering and the MS degree in computer science from the Middle East Technical University, Ankara, Turkey, in 1972 and 1974, respectively, and the PhD degree in computing science from the University of Alberta, Edmonton, Alberta, Canada, in 1980.
He is presently a Professor of Computer Engineering and Science, Case Western Reserve University, Cleveland, OH. His research interests are in databases and multimedia computing.

Multimedia Tools and Applications, 4, 199–223 (1997)

Management of Multi-structured Hypermedia Documents : A Data Model, Query Language, and Indexing Scheme*

KYUCHUL LEE kclee@comeng.chungnam.ac.kr
Department of Computer Engineering, Chungnam National University, 220 Kung-dong, Yoosung-ku, Taejon, KOREA 305-764

YONG KYU LEE yklee@cat.syr.edu
Research and Development Group, Korea Telecom Seoul, KOREA 137-792

P. BRUCE BERRA berra@cat.syr.edu
Department of Electrical Engineering and Computer Science, Syracuse University, Syracuse, NY 13244-4100

Abstract. Structured documents have gained popularity with the advent of document structure markup standards such as SGML, ODA, HyTime, and HTML. Document management systems can provide powerful facilities by maintaining the structure information of documents. Since the hypermedia document is also a kind of structured document, we can apply the results of many studies, which have been performed in storing, retrieving, and managing structured documents, to the hypermedia document management.

However, more factors should be considered in handling hypermedia documents because they contain multimedia data and also have multiple complex structures such as hyperlink networks and spatial/temporal layout structures as well as logical structures.

In this paper, we propose an object-oriented model for multi-structured hypermedia documents and multimedia data, and a query language for retrieving hypermedia document elements based on the content and multiple complex structures. By using unique element identifiers and an indexing scheme which exploits multiple structures, we can process queries efficiently with minimal storage overhead for maintaining structure information.

Keywords: structured documents, hypertext, multimedia, object-oriented databases, query languages

1. Introduction

The document is one of the most important media in representing, understanding, communicating, and disseminating information. With rapid growth in the use of computers to process information, the problem of how to store and retrieve documents is becoming increasingly important.

Structured documents are complex and compound documents that consist of units of information of a finer granularity than traditional flat file-based documents. Structured documents have gained popularity with the advent of document structure markup standards such as SGML(Standard Generalized Markup Language) [14], ODA(Office Doc-

* This work was supported by the Korea Science and Engineering Foundation.

ument Architecture) [13], HyTime(Hypermedia/Time-Based Structuring Language) [15], and HTML(HyperText Markup Language) used in the World-Wide Web.

Document management systems can provide powerful facilities by maintaining the structure information of documents. For example, maintaining the structure information makes it possible to pose structure queries based on the logical structure of documents such as chapters, sections, or paragraphs. The structure information also provides many advantages for authors and readers to edit, organize, and understand document content.

However, traditional text retrieval systems present a significant disadvantage when used as a structured document management system because they cannot share, reuse, query, and manage any of the structural units in the document [22]. Therefore, much research in storing and retrieving structured documents using database systems has been performed[2] [4] [9] [22].

The research issues, which have been studied in the structured document management, include :

- what kinds of data models to use for modeling structure information effectively
- how to express queries for retrieving structure elements
- how to develop appropriate indexing structures for supporting fast structure element access.

On the other hand, multimedia documents have recently received a lot of attention due to advances in multimedia computing environments such as high-speed networks, new storage media, and multimedia presentation devices. Multimedia documents can support the dynamic composition of multimedia data including audio, video, graphics, and images as well as text. By combining multimedia documents and hypertext technology, we can build more powerful hypermedia documents.

Most previous studies about structured document management [2] [4] [9] [22] have focused on text-oriented documents. The basic idea of this paper stems from the fact that structure information plays as important a role in managing and handling hypermedia documents as it does in text-oriented documents. In managing hypermedia documents, more structures have to be considered. An ideal hypermedia document representation must allow multiple structures including the layout(or physical) structure as well as the logical structure. The layout structure specifies the layout of the components actually presented to the user on output devices, while the logical structure represents the hierarchical structure between logical elements.

We can further classify the layout structure into the spatial layout structure and the temporal layout structure. The temporal layout structure is not required in text-oriented documents. However, it is essential for multimedia documents to present the components of a document in a coherent, synchronized manner according to the author's intention. For instance, audio must accompany the image presented synchronously in slide presentations.

One more structure for hypermedia documents is the hyperlink network. It is formed by interlinking related documents to each other.

In this paper, we propose solutions in data modeling, query language, and index structures for multi-structured hypermedia documents. In representing multi-structured documents, the object-oriented data modeling technique is used since the structure information has hierarchical characteristics. Furthermore, our scheme models all the document structures and includes multimedia data modeling, which makes it possible to share multimedia content between structures.

Our query language supports four types of queries : attribute query, content query, structure query, and hyperlink query. We can also make more powerful mixed queries of the four types. The query language syntax follows the ODMG-93 standard [6], and the query expressions are enriched to support efficient description of document structures and hyperlink traversal. Queries can be posed based on any combination of logical, spatial layout, temporal layout, and hyperlink network structures. To our knowledge, this functionality can not be supported by previous work.

In order to perform structure queries efficiently, index structures that support fast element access must be provided because users want to access all kinds of document elements in the database. However, in the previous systems, little attention has been focused on structured document indexing. In this paper, we propose a new indexing scheme which supports not only processing structure queries efficiently but also reducing the storage overhead of indices considerably. Our scheme exploits the hierarchical document structures and uses the fact that index terms are inherited between hierarchically related elements.

This paper is organized as follows. In Section 2, a typical example of the multi-structured hypermedia document is described, and multi-structural aspects of hypermedia documents are explained. Multi-structure information and multimedia data are modeled based on the object-oriented data model in Section 3. The query language is described in Section 4, and a new indexing scheme for efficient accessing multi-structured hypermedia documents is proposed in Section 5. In Section 6, we describe and compare our approach with previous work. Finally, Section 7 presents the conclusions and comments about future work.

2. Multi-structured Hypermedia Document

This section gives a detailed example of a multi-structured hypermedia document, and explains characteristics of each document structure. The sample document, a hypermedia document about the CASE center at Syracuse University, is presented in Figure 1.

It consists of text portions such as the title, the author, an abstract, and several paragraphs. It can include other multimedia data such as video, images, audio, and graphics. The document can be interlinked to other documents which may have the same document type or different document types. In this example, the anchors of links are underlined, however, other symbols(e.g. icons) could be used.

The logical structure, which forms a hierarchical representation of a document, represents how to construct a document by a set of logical elements such as title, section, and paragraph. It makes it easier for the reader to understand the contents. Therefore, most of the document standards(e.g. SGML, ODA) provide schemes for representing the logical structure. Figure 2 shows a SGML DTD(Document Type Definition) for our hypermedia article example. The DTD contains element definitions that describe sub-elements and the content model which elements can have. The following is the marked-up sample hypermedia article, which is

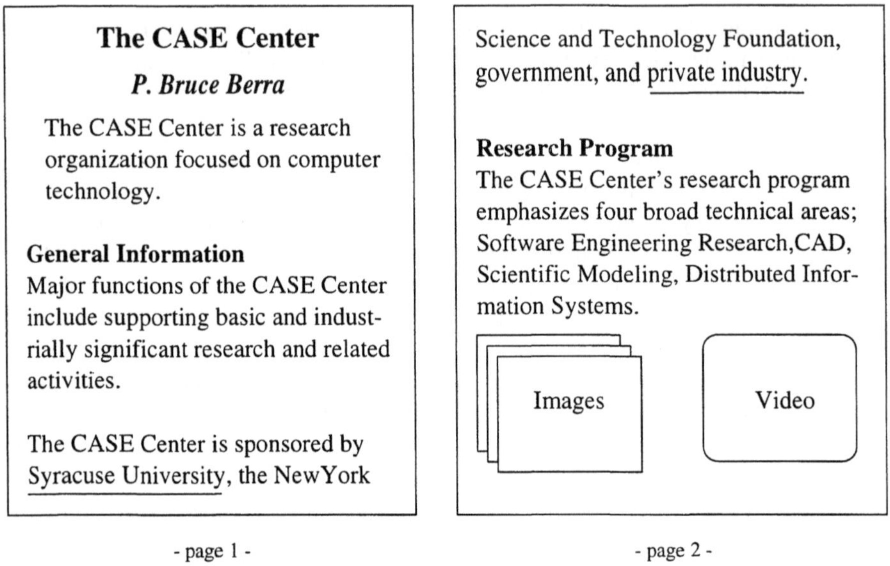

Figure 1. A sample of hypermedia article

presented in Figure 1. This sample article is composed of logical structure elements defined in the DTD in Figure 2.

```
<hm_article>
<title> The CASE Center </title>
<author> P. Bruce Berra </author>
<abstract> The CASE Center ........  technology. </abstract>
<section>
<sectitle> General Information </sectitle>
<body>
<paragraph>
Major functions  .........     activities.
</paragraph>
<paragraph>
Our Center is sponsored by <link linkend=syr.sgml> Syracuse University </link>,
the NewYork Science and Technology Foundation, government, and
<link linkend=private.sgml> private industry </link> .
</paragraph>
</body>
</section>
<section>
<sectitle> Research Program </sectitle>
<body>
<paragraph> The CASE  .........
.............      Systems.
</paragraph>
<image source=overview.gif     format=gif>  </image>
<image source=compappl.jpeg    format=jpeg> </image>
<image source=softeng.gif      format=gif>  </image>
```

```
<!DOCTYPE   hm_article  [
<!ELEMENT   hm_article  - -  (title, author+, abstract, section+)>
<!ATTLIST   hm_article  rev_date  CDATA  #IMPLIED>
<!ELEMENT   title       - -  (#PCDATA)>
<!ELEMENT   author      - o  (#PCDATA)>
<!ELEMENT   abstract    - o  (#PCDATA)>
<!ELEMENT   section     - o  (sectitle, body)>
<!ELEMENT   sectitle    - o  (#PCDATA)>
<!ELEMENT   body        - o  (paragraph | image | video | graphic | audio)*>
<!ELEMENT   paragraph   - o  (#PCDATA | link*)>
<!ELEMENT   link        - -  (#PCDATA)>
<!ATTLIST   link        linkend  CDATA  #REQUIRED>
<!ELEMENT   (image, video, graphic, audio)  - -  EMPTY>
<!ATTLIST   (image, video, graphic, audio)
                        source   CDATA  #REQUIRED
                        format   CDATA  #REQUIRED>  ]>
```

Figure 2. A DTD for hypermedia articles

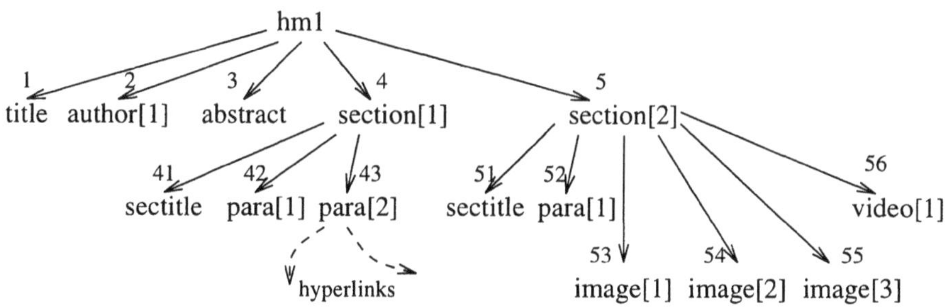

Figure 3. A composite object for the logical structure of the sample document

```
<video source=reseacharea.mpeg format=mpeg> </video>
</body>
</section>
</hm_article>
```

In the logical structure hierarchy of a document, a document is composed of child components. For instance, the title, the author, an abstract, and two sections in Figure 3 are aggregated to form a hypermedia document composite object "$hm1$" of the type $HM\_Article$ defined in Figure 2. There is a $part\text{-}of$ relationship between a child node and a parent node. In a composite object, the document itself is the root of the hierarchy, and only leaf nodes contain text or multimedia data.

The layout structure describes the hierarchical aggregation structure of presentation components of a document. We can further classify the layout structure into the spatial layout structure and the temporal layout structure as mentioned in the last section. For an example

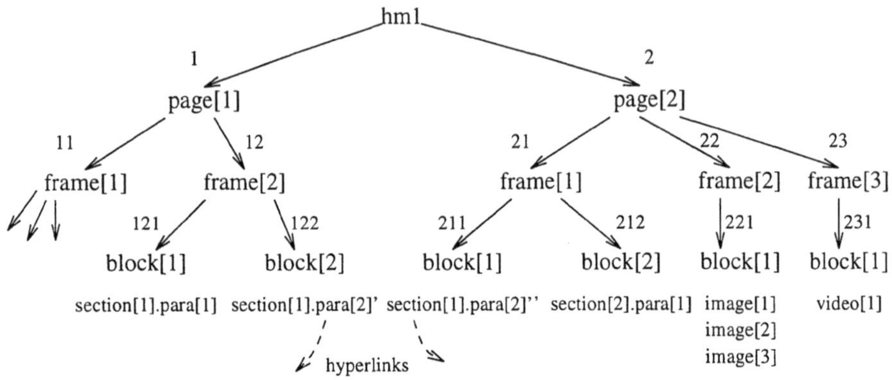

Figure 4. A composite object for the spatial layout structure of the sample document

of the temporal layout information, we need a scenario to present synchronously three images in the left image frame and one video clip in the right video frame in the page number 2 of the document in Figure 1 even though we know the presentation position of each frame.

A spatial layout composite object for a document consists of a set of *pages*. A *page* is composed of rectangular areas called *frames*, and there may be several *blocks* that contain multimedia data in a frame(Figure 4). We use the ODA terminologies to represent spatial layout structure elements. However, it does not mean that our scheme is dependent on a specific document model. Even though the SGML standard does not support the layout structure, it can be produced during the formatting process by a formatter or typesetter.

The content of a leaf logical object does not always correspond to the content of a layout block. The logical object *section*[1].*para*[2] is divided into two portions(i.e. *section*[1].*para*[2]′ and *section*[1].*para*[2]″) and associated with two separate blocks, that is *page*[1].*frame*[2].*block*[2] and *page*[2].*frame*[1].*block*[1], belonging to two different pages as shown in Figure 1, 3, and 4. On the other hand, several logical objects(i.e., *image*[1],*image*[2],*image*[3]) can fit into one layout block *page*[2].*frame*[2].*block*[1] in a spatial layout structure.

To represent the temporal layout structure, we use the temporal relationship specification scheme developed by the first author of this paper [17]. Allen [1] has defined 13 temporal relations between two time intervals. These temporal relations are: *before*, *meets*, *during*, *overlaps*, *starts*, *finishes*, and *equal* plus their inverse relations(except *equal*). In [17], the delay object, a special kind of object representing specified delay, is introduced to represent Allen's 13 temporal relations simply as a composition hierarchy of two types of relationship, namely the *parallel*(*par*) and *sequential*(*seq*) relationships, without any loss of semantics. For example, Allen's "finishes(A,B)" relation can be interpreted as a parallel relationship between two objects, that is one object is a sequential composition of a delay object *d* and an object A and the other is an object B. Therefore, this relation can be represented in our scheme as "par(seq(d,A), B)".

Let's assume that the author's intention of the presentation of *page*[2] in the document "*hm*1" is the timeline diagram as shown in Figure 5. Note that the logical object *video*[1] is

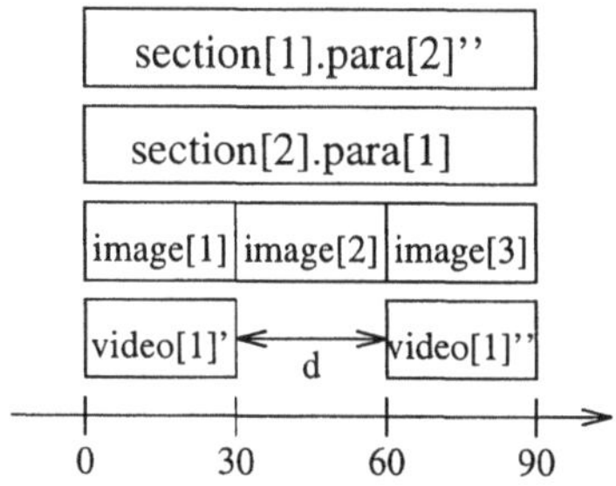

Figure 5. A timeline diagram for presenting schedule of page 2 of the sample document

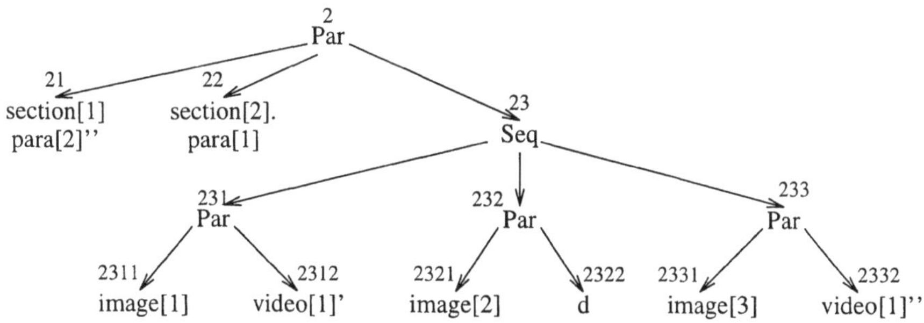

Figure 6. A complex object for the temporal layout structure of the sample document

divided into two fragments(i.e. $video[1]'$ and $video[1]''$) which have the same presentation time with a 30-second delay between them. They are synchronized with two text blocks and three images in presentation.

Figure 6 represents a composite object hierarchy for this presentation schedule. The 30-second delay between video fragments is treated as an object, and has a $parallel$ relationship with the object $image[2]$.

3. Object-Oriented Modeling of Structure Information

The object-oriented DBMS technology has been popular because it is best suited to meet the requirements of advanced applications which include multimedia information systems and document management systems. It can be used to model the complex hierarchical structures of hypermedia documents. In addition, the classification, generalization, and aggregation relationships between document objects can be directly supported by the object-oriented DBMS.

Figure 7 illustrates the type hierarchy designed for document structures. There are three abstract subtypes of the type $Doc\_Structure$ - the first subtype Doc_Type modeling the different kinds of documents(e.g., memos, hypermedia articles), the second subtype $Structure\_Type$ modeling the categories of structures(e.g., logical, spatial layout, tempo-

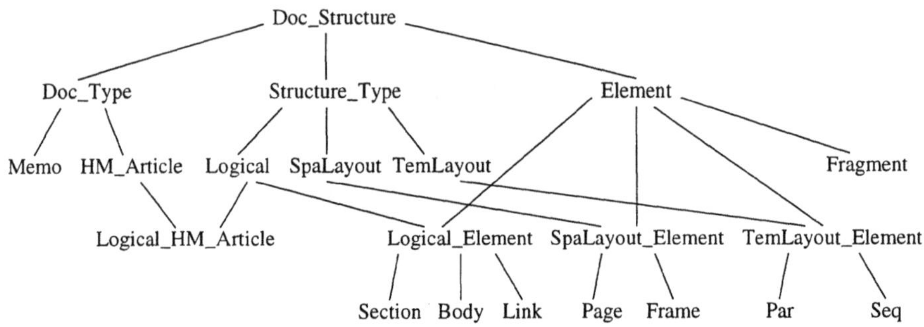

Figure 7. The type hierarchy for hypermedia document structures

ral layout), and the third subtype *Element* modeling all the elements of three structures. The structure of a document is defined as a subtype of two subtypes of *Doc_Type* and *Structure_Type*. For example, the type *Logical_HM_Article* representing the logical structure of *HM_Article* has two supertypes *HM_Article* and *Logical*.

Every element of these structures is represented by a type. For instances, the *section* element in the logical structure is represented by the type *Section*, and the *page* element in the spatial layout structure is modeled as the type *Page*. Each element type is classified into three categories as shown in Figure 7 according to the structural aspects. The type *Fragment* represents multimedia data contents which are leaf nodes in composite object for each structure.

3.1. Representation of Hierarchical Structure Information

In order to support queries on multiple document structures, we have to maintain the information about the composite object for each structure. Previously, database relations [7], parse trees [4], and element locators [2] have been used. However, they require considerable space and disk access time. In this paper, we propose a novel scheme which uses specially designed unique element identifiers (UID's) for structure queries. By letting the UID carry information about the document structure, the UID's of the ancestor or descendant nodes of a node can be obtained directly from the UID.

Our scheme uses the tree location address of the HyQ [16] as the UID. In the tree location address, a node address in a hierarchy is the concatenation of the children identifiers in the path from the root to the node. For example, the tree location address of the node which is the fourth child of the third child of the second child of the root is '1234'. In our scheme, we use '234' as the UID of the node and do not include the root identifier which is always '1'.

The number associated with each node in Figure 3,4,6 is the UID. We use three UIDs – *lid*(logical object UID), *sid*(spatial layout object UID), and *tid*(temporal layout object UID) – for each element of three structures. The object key of an element consists of its UID and the *doc_id* of the document which the element belongs to. Each of the at-

```
interface Logical_HM_Article : HM_Article, Logical {
      keys  doc_id;
// Attributes inherited from Doc_Type
attribute string   doc_id;
attribute Text     text_content;
// Attributes defined here
attribute Date     rev_date;
attribute TextFragment title;
attribute List<TextFragment> authors;
attribute TextFragment abstract;
attribute List<Section> sections;}
```

Figure 8. The type definition of *Logical_HM_Article*

tributes *lid*, *sid*, and *tid* is defined in the type *Logical_Element*,*SpLayout_Element*, and *TemLayout_Element*, respectively.

The UID of the parent node of a node whose UID is i can be obtained by shifting one digit right as follows:

$$parent(i) = shift\_right(i) \tag{1}$$

The UID of the j-th child node of a node whose UID is i can be obtained by shifting one digit left after concatenating i with j as follows:

$$child(i, j) = shift\_left(concatenate(i, j)) \tag{2}$$

The operations, *parent* and *child*, are defined in the type *Doc_Structure* as *methods*, and inherited by all element types and used to locate ancestor and descendant objects fast without looking up additional information.

3.2. Type Definition for Structure Information

Figure 8 presents the type definition of *Logical_HM_Article* corresponding to the logical element definition in the DTD of Figure 2. The definition of type is specified as compliant with the ODMG-93 [6], which is the standard for accessing object-oriented databases.

In the definition, the attribute *doc_id* is declared for identifying a document uniquely, and the attribute *text_content* has an object identifier of the text object containing the entire text content of a document. These attributes are defined in the type *Doc_Type* and inherited by its subtypes. The method *GetDoc*() is also defined in the type *Doc_Type* in order to obtain the entire document content at once. The reason that we treat the text content as a whole will be explained in the next subsection.

The attribute *rev_date* is a descriptive attribute, while the other four attributes – *title*, *authors*, *abstract*, and *sections* – represent the logical structure elements. Note that we define the attribute *sections* by using a one-way aggregation relationship instead of a two-way relationship like: "relationship List<Section> sections inverse Section::is_section_of". If the aggregation relationship is defined as a two-way relationship, it is possible to traverse

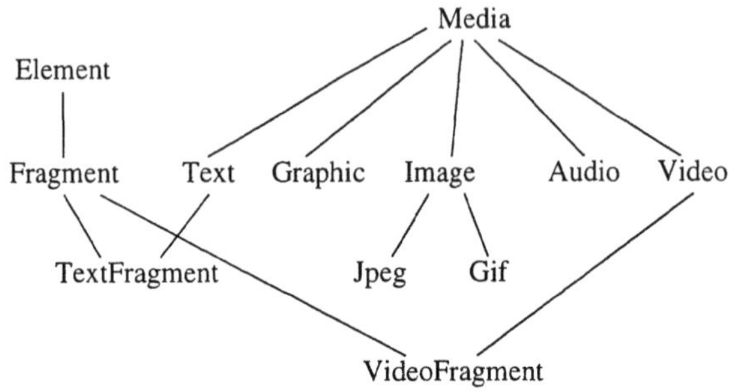

Figure 9. The type hierarchy for multimedia data

parent and child objects in a composite hierarchy by following the *parent-child links*. However, it is required to access all intermediate objects if we want to retrieve an ancestor object of an object when the difference of levels between them is greater than 1. By using our UID scheme and *parent*, *child* functions, we do not have to maintain two-way *parent-child links* and do not need to access all the objects between them. Therefore, it provides great advantages in minimizing the storage space for *parent-child links* and in enhancing the performance of accessing ancestors and descendants of an object at any level.

3.3. *Modeling of Multimedia Data*

Various kinds of multimedia data can be supported in our system(Figure 9). Multimedia data are instances of the type *Media*, and hold the raw data along with other attributes for presentation such as *position* for spatial presentation, and *start*(*time*) and *end*(*time*) for temporal presentation. Each media type(e.g. *Image*) can have subtypes(e.g., *Jpeg*, *Gif*) according to its data format.

Methods for editing and querying can be implemented in each media type. For simplicity, we assume that content queries on multimedia data are based on conventional information retrieval techniques, which search given keywords in the text description or captions or annotations associated with multimedia data. However, it is possible to use media specific search methods implemented in each media type to pose queries. For example, the query, "select documents with images whose colors are blue," uses the color feature extraction method defined in the type *Image*.

The actual data of each media type is stored as a BLOB(binary large object) in our framework even if the media type is *Text*. Each leaf object does not contain actual data. Instead, it contains the pointer to the original source data(i.e. BLOB data) and the list of *offset* denoting the start position within the source data and *length* in bytes. This type of object is modeled as the type *Fragment*, which is a subtype of the type *Element* in Figure 9.

For example, the second paragraph of the first section of a hypermedia document "$hm1$" in Figure 1 consists of two text fragments because the paragraph is divided into two blocks after the layout processing is completed. The two text fragment objects are shown below.

```
text_fragment5 [doc_id:"hm1", source:text1,
                lid:43, sid:122, tid:11, offset:<(146,50)>]
text_fragment6 [doc_id:"hm1", source:text1,
                lid:43, sid:211, tid:21, offset:<(196,90)>]
```

The system can know that two objects belong to the same logical paragraph since they have the same lid. However, they are presented in different pages and synchronized with other data as they have different sids and tids.

For another example, the object $video[1]$ in Figure 3 and 4 is divided into two video clips when they are presented as shown in Figure 5. In this case, there is no problem even if some portions of video clips overlap because they are implemented as two video fragment objects and are not stored in duplicate.

Many benefits can be obtained by treating multimedia data in this manner:

- This scheme can be easily implemented because most of the object-oriented DBMS's support the BLOB data type.
- Retrieving the whole text content of a document can be achieved efficiently since we don't have to join partitioned texts together.
- The composite objects for multiple structures can share the data content of leaf nodes, and it provides flexibility to accommodate the structure changes.
- Data duplication can be avoided when an element instance is nested in another element instance. For example, an anchor string of a link can be represented by a text fragment object; otherwise, the string value of the link should be stored in duplicate.
- As highlighted in the above video example, a certain portion of multimedia data can be shared between multiple element objects.

Updating the text contents or changing multimedia data could be considered a disadvantage of this approach because the fragment offsets should be changed. However, we assume that the document archive is relatively static. In this environment, updates can be performed in a batch mode rather than an interactive mode.

4. The Query Language

We provide the following four types of queries which should be supported for multi-structured hypermedia documents.

- Attribute queries : queries based on attributes(e.g., doc_id, rev_date).

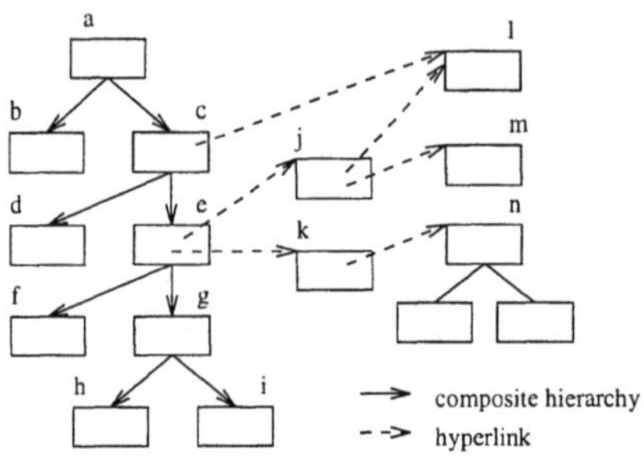

Figure 10. Example document composite object and hyperlink network

- Content queries : queries based on the document contents which include text and multimedia data
- Structure queries : queries based on the logical, spatial/temporal layout structural elements
- Hyperlink queries : queries based on the hyperlink networks

We can also make more powerful mixed queries of the above four types. Syntax of the Query Language for Structured Hypermedia Document(QLSHD) of this paper, a modified version of the query language of [18], follows the OQL(Object Query Language) of the ODMG-93 standard [6], and the query expressions of QLSHD are enriched to support efficient description of document structures and hyperlink traversal.

4.1. Basic Expressions

In QLSHD, users specify required document elements using a document expression. The document expression is defined as follows [18].

- A document expression is of the form $d.P$, where d is a document variable and P is a path expression or a group of path expressions connected by a dot(.).
- A path expression can be a branch expression, link expression, or list expression.

An example of the document composite object and hyperlink network for demonstrating the query expressions is illustrated in Figure 10.

The branch expression allows navigating to ancestor or descendant elements of an element through document's specific structures. The syntax of branch expression is $branch[parameter]$, where $parameter$ specifies the number of hops to navigate forwards or backwards. The $parameters$ are defined as follows:

```
* : 0 or more hops forward          / : 0 or more hops backward
+ : 1 or more hops forward          - : 1 or more hops backward
```

```
0 : no hop
> : hops to leaf nodes              < : hops to root node
i : i hops forward                 -i : i hops backward
i - j : i - j hops forward         -i - -j : i - j hops backward
```

The following show some examples of the branch expression for Figure 10.

```
e.branch[*]={e,f,g,h,i}            e.branch[-]={a,c}
e.branch[>]={h,i}                  e.branch[1-2]={f,g,h,i}
```

The link expression makes the hypertext navigation possible. We can specify not only the navigation of 0 or more hops through the hyperlinks but also forward/backward traversal. The link expression is defined similarly as the branch expression like $link[parameter]$.

The following show some examples of the link expressions for Figure 10.

```
e.link[+]={j,k,l,m,n}              l.link[-]={c,e,j}
e.link[1-2]={j,k,l,m,n}            l.link[-2]={e}
```

The list expression is designed to locate a specific portion of a list of elements. It is defined as follows:

- Either L[i] or L[i:j] is a list expression, where L is an element name, branch expression, or link expression, and i and j are integers or character '>'. L[i] returns the i-th element, or the last element in the case of '>', from the list L. L[i:j] extracts the sublist of L starting at position i and ending at position j.

Examples of the list expression are given below.

```
sections[2].paragraphs[>]: the last paragraph of the second section
sections[1:3]: the first, the second, and the third sections
branch[1][2]: the second child of an object in the hierarchy
```

The branch expression, link expression, and list expression can be combined to make more powerful path expressions. The following examples show combined expressions for the document graph in Figure 10.

```
a.branch[2][2].link[1]={j,k}          e.link[1][2].link[-1]={e}
l.link[-1][1].branch[1]={d,e}         e.branch[-2][1]={b}
k.link[-1].branch[+]={f,g,h,i}
```

Example queries on the logical structure using the branch, link, and list expressions are given below.

- Select sections that have any sub-element containing the keyword "research".

  select s

  from h **in** hm_articles

  where exists s **in** h.sections:(s.branch[*].**contains**("research"))

- Select all memos which refer to hm_articles whose titles contain "CASE" and "Center".

  select m

  from h **in** hm_articles, m **in** memos

  where h.title.**contains**("CASE" **and** "Center") **and** m **in** h.link[-]

- Select the titles of hm_articles that are referenced by the last child of the second section of the hm_article "hm1".

  select k.title

  from (h,k) **in** hm_articles, s **in** h.sections[2]

  where h.doc_id="hm1" **and** k **in** s.branch[1][>].link[1]

4.2. Queries Based on Multi-structure of the Document

Example queries shown in the last subsection are based on the logical structure of the hypermedia document. Since hypermedia documents are modeled to have multiple structures in our scheme, queries based on other structures can be posed.

Queries about the spatial layout structure are similar to queries about the logical structure except the elements consisting of the spatial layout hierarchy are different. For example, the query "select hm_articles that have pages containing the keywords 'CASE' and 'Center'." is expressed in QLSHD as follows:

select h

from h **in** hm_articles

where exists p **in** h.pages:(p.**contains**("CASE" **and** "Center"))

Queries can be posed without a precise knowledge of the spatial layout structure. For example, the query, "select all blocks presented on the same page with a video block.", can be represented in QLSHD as follows:

select p.branch[>]

from h **in** hm_articles, p **in** h.pages

where exists b **in** p.branch[>]:((Video)b)

In the above query, the expression $(Video)b$ asserts that b is an object of the type $Video$. If it turns out that it is not true, an exception is raised at runtime [6]. This is useful for identifying the type of an object when it is an instance of the type that has two or more supertypes like the type $VideoFragment$ in Figure 9. This query returns the set of blocks which are presented on the same page with the video block. In our example of Figure 4, two text blocks, three image blocks, and a video block are returned as a result. This kind of query cannot be processed if we only maintain the logical structure information.

We can also make more powerful queries by using combinations of branch, link, and list expressions. The following show query examples based on the spatial layout structure.

- Select the pages of hm_articles that have any sub-element containing the keyword "research".

  select p

  from h **in** hm_articles

  where exists p **in** h.pages:(p.branch[*].**contains**("research"))

- Select the memos referenced directly or indirectly by the page two of a hm_article whose doc_id is "hm1".

  select m

  from h **in** hm_articles, p **in** h.pages[2], m **in** memos

  where h.doc_id="hm1" **and** (m **in** p.link[+])

- Select the first blocks(i.e. title) of hm_articles that are referenced by the last block of the first page of the hm_article "hm1".

  select k.branch[>][1]

  from (h,k) **in** hm_articles, p **in** h.pages[1]

  where h.doc_id = "hm1" **and** k **in** p.branch[2][>].link[1]

Queries based on the temporal layout structure are focused on the temporal relationships between presented objects. As shown in Figure 6, the synchronization relationships are represented by a hierarchical structure between the media instances. The following example shows a typical temporal structure query.

- Select the blocks of hm_articles presented in parallel and equal duration with a block containing the keyword "Science".

  select c

  from h **in** hm_articles, (b,c) **in** h.branch[>]

  where c.**equal**(b) **and** b.**contains**("Science")

The above query uses $equal()$ operation defined in the type $Media$. It is inherited by each media fragment types because they are subtypes of the type $Media$. The expression $c.equal(b)$ tests whether objects c and b have an $equal$ temporal relationship. If it holds, then it returns $true$. The answer of the query will be the object $video[1]''$, that is the second half of $video[1]$, if we assume that the object $image[3]$ contains the keyword "Science" in Figure 5. The method $equal$ is actually implemented in QLSHD expression like : "c.start=b.start and c.end=b.end and (Par)(c.branch[-1] intersect b.branch[-1])". The attributes $start$ and end denote the starting and ending coordinates in presenting a media object. In this expression, one may think that the clause "c.start=b.start and c.end=b.end" is sufficient to specify the $equal$ relationship condition, but the clause "(Par)(c.branch[-1] intersect b.branch[-1])" reduces the expensive value joins between each $start$ and end attributes of all blocks because it limits the search space to the objects which have the common parent object whose type is Par.

Another similar example is given below.

- Select the blocks of hm_articles presented just before an image containing the keyword "CAD".

  select c

  from h **in** hm_articles, (b,c) **in** h.branch[>]

  where c.**meets**(b) **and** b.**contains**("CAD") **and** (Image)b

The expression $c.meets(b)$ in the above query means it is $true$ when there is $meets$ relationship between c and b objects. In other words, c is presented just before b without any gap. If we assume that the image object containing the keyword "CAD" is $image[2]$ in Figure 5, the result will be a set of $image[1]$ and $video[1]'$.

We need to implement operations for all Allen's [1] thirteen temporal relationships between two intervals of objects in order to support temporal structure queries. However, only seven operations(i.e., $before$, $meets$, $during$, $overlaps$, $starts$, $finishes$, and $equal$) are implemented because the thirteen relationships can be represented by seven cases since six of them are inverses. For example, $after$ is the inverse relationship of $before$(a $equals$ b is the same as b $equals$ a). The inverse operations can be represented using the non-inverse operations only by exchanging the arguments. These operations can also be used for finding n-ary temporal relationships because they test all objects in a presentation scenario iteratively.

It is possible to make queries based on the combination of the three structures. These queries will be explained in Section 5.2.

5. Indexing Multi-structured Hypermedia Documents

In this section, we propose a new indexing scheme which supports not only processing structure queries efficiently but also reducing the storage overhead of indices considerably.

5.1. Optimizing Inverted Indices

The inverted index [23] [10] has been used by many information retrieval systems for efficient accessing full-text data. A term's inverted list stores a document identifier for every document in which the term appears.

In order to support direct element access for performing structure queries efficiently, it is also required to include all the index terms of elements in the inverted index. In the composite object hierarchy, leaf nodes are associated with data while internal nodes represent only structure relationships between document elements. Suppose that a document has three leaf nodes and each leaf element has index terms as shown in Figure 11 (a). Here, we can consider the node A is a chapter, B and C are sections, and D and E are paragraphs.

Even though the internal nodes have no associated document data, the data at the subtrees must be considered as their data. Thus, the index terms for each node are as follows:

```
index(A) = {mammal,pet,cow,cat,dog}
index(B) = {mammal,pet,cat,dog}
```

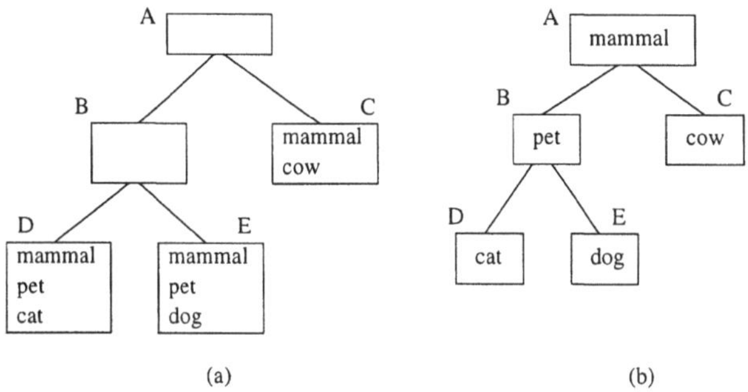

Figure 11. Document composite object : (a) leaf nodes with index terms (b) indices without replication

```
index(C) = {mammal,cow}
index(D) = {mammal,pet,cat}
index(E) = {mammal,pet,dog}
```

Now the problem is how to maintain an inverted index structure for fast access to document elements. We propose a novel method of building the inverted list which saves considerable space. Figure 11 (b) shows how to build an index for structured documents using the fact that the child nodes of a node can have some index terms in common. The inverted list for the example is as follows:

```
inverted-list(mammal) = {A}        inverted-list(pet) = {B}
inverted-list(cow) = {C}           inverted-list(cat) = {D}
inverted-list(dog) = {E}
```

In this scheme, the index of a node is

$$\text{INDEX[node]} \cup \text{INDEX[ancestors]} \cup \text{INDEX[descendents]}.$$

That is, the index terms of the internal nodes are inherited by their descendant nodes. Using this inverted index scheme, we can access any element in the database using the *parent* and *child* function with much less index space.

The number of document identifiers in an inverted list increases dramatically as the number of document elements, in which the index term appears, is getting larger. Intuitively, the index size of our scheme(Figure 11 (b)) decreases if the rate of promoted keywords from child nodes to parent nodes increases. However, the index size of the traditional scheme(Figure 11 (a)) does not change because common keywords do not contribute to a decrease in the number of entries in the inverted list.

The extensive analysis results [19] of our approach compared with other indexing schemes show that the storage requirements are minimized and the performance of accessing an element is enhanced.

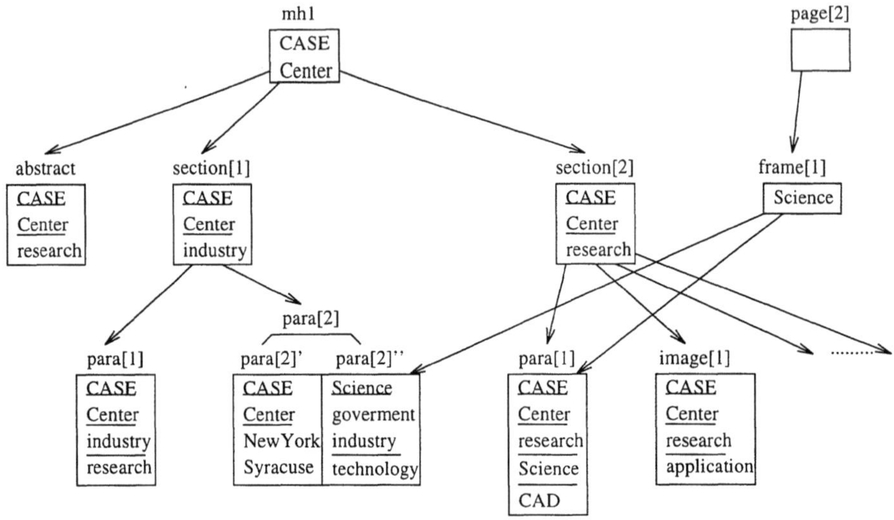

Figure 12. The partial logical/spatial layout hierarchy with index terms for the sample document

5.2. Multi-structure Inverted Index

Our indexing scheme exploits the hierarchical document structure and uses the fact that index terms are inherited between hierarchically related elements. We can obtain greater benefits when this scheme is applied to the spatial and temporal layout structures as well as the logical structure.

In Figure 12, we show the partial logical and spatial layout hierarchy of the sample document in Figure 1. The index terms in leaf nodes are extracted from each text object and multimedia object. The common terms that are underlined become the index terms of the parent node. For example, the terms – "CASE", "Center", and "industry" – are common in $para[1]$ and $para[2]$ of $section[1]$, and they become index terms for the whole section.

Index terms for the whole logical document are "CASE" and "Center" because they are common in the abstract and two sections. The inverted list for the common keywords of the example is as follows:

```
inverted-list(CASE) = {hm1}
inverted-list(Center) = {hm1}
inverted-list(research) = {abstract,section[1].para[1],section[2]}
inverted-list(industry) = {section[1]}
inverted-list(science) = {page[2].frame[1]}
```

As you can see in this example, common keywords are not hard to find because all the elements of a document tend to focus on a common topic. This phenomenon can be more easily found between adjacent elements such as paragraphs of a section or frames on a page.

In other words, common terms are localized, and document elements, which have common concepts, are clustered in the document.

This characteristic makes it possible to build more efficient index structures. The paragraphs $section[1].para[2]''$ and $section[2].para[1]$ in Figure 12 have no common keywords when we consider only the logical structure. However, we can find a common keyword "Science" if the spatial layout structure is taken into account.

Using this index scheme, some queries can be processed very fast, and we can also pose queries based on the multi-structure. An example query which show this advantage is given below.

- Select sections containing the keyword "CASE" and "Center" in the hm_article "hm1".

  select s

  from h **in** hm_articles, s **in** h.sections

  where h.doc_id = "hm1" **and** s.**contains**("CASE" **and** "Center")

In the case of having only an inverted index for leaf objects, all the object identifiers pointed by the index entries of "CASE" or "Center" must be accessed and ANDed. Then the result objects have to be retrieved to find their sections. However, the only thing we have to do in our scheme is to return section identifiers of the document "$hm1$" because we know that the only index entry satisfying the query condition is exactly "$hm1$" without retrieving any sub-elements.

The next query example is to retrieve the spatial layout elements based on the logical elements.

- Select pages presenting sections whose all elements have the keyword "industry".

  select p

  from h **in** hm_articles, p **in** h.pages, s **in** h.sections

  where for all x **in** s.branch[>]:x.**contains**("industry") **and** p **in** x.branch[-2]

This query shows that it is possible to search the layout elements related to a certain logical element. We can also search the logical elements based on the layout elements and vice versa. The above query can be processed very fast because $section[2]$ has a common keyword "industry" in all its paragraphs.

The following query example demonstrates that we can pose a query on temporal relationships combined with other structure information.

- Select elements that start presentation with a paragraph containing the keyword "CAD".

  select t

  from h **in** hm_articles, pa **in** h.paragraphs, t **in** h.branch[>]

  where pa.**contains**("CAD") **and** pa.**starts**(t)

The query returns two text objects $section[1].para[2]''$ and $section[2].para[1]$), a video object(i.e. $video[1]'$), and an image object(i.e. $image[1]$).

5.3. *Indexing and Querying Structured Multimedia Data*

Some multimedia data such as graphics, animation, video, and music have inherent hierarchical structures [12]. We can consider the application of our schemes to such structured multimedia data because they have structures like documents. For example, a video clip can consist of one or more segments, a segment can consist of one or more events, and an event can consist of one or more shots. Our query language and indexing scheme can be used to manage and handle the structure information of structured multimedia data.

In order to obtain keywords from video structure elements, we can use user annotations or captions. Users can freely annotate video elements with text data and keywords can be extracted from the text data. Other methods can also be used. For example, automated video analysis tools can be used to extract keywords from video frames.

Since a video clip has a hierarchical structure, we can interpret the nodes of Figure 11 as video elements. For example, we can assume that the node A is a segment, B and C are events, and D and E are shots. Thus, we can construct the same index structure for video data and we can treat video data as text documents.

Queries also can be posed based on the structure of video data. Example queries on the structure of video data are given below.

- Select segments that have an event about "waterfall".

  select s

  from v **in** video

  where exists s **in** v.segments:(s.events.**contains**("waterfall"))

- Select all audio nodes referenced by the memos which have a link to a video node.

  select a

  from a **in** audio, m **in** memos, v **in** video

  where a **in** m.link[1] **and** m **in** v.link[-1]

6. Related Work

Much research have been performed on modeling structures of documents [2] [3] [5] [9] [20] [22]. Most of the models are based on the object-oriented modeling techniques since the structure information has hierarchical characteristics and current structured document standards such as SGML, ODA, HyTime, and HTML also use the object-oriented concept.

Compared with the previous models, our modeling scheme is not dependent on any specific document standard. It is also not closely related to a specific DBMS implementation. Furthermore, our scheme models all the document structures and includes multimedia data modeling, which makes it possible to share multimedia content between structures.

Query languages for structured documents should support content-based access and structure-based access [22]. Our query language supports four types of queries: attribute query, content query, structure query, and hyperlink query. We can also make more powerful mixed queries of the four types. Furthermore, we have proposed queries based on any combination of logical, spatial layout, temporal layout, and hyperlink network structures. To our knowledge, this functionality can not be supported by previous work.

Arnold-Moore et al. [2] have presented a data model and query language for the SGML documents. They have defined a functional query language, called SGQL, which supports structure queries as well as content queries. However, the SGQL is not user-friendly for complex structure queries because it requires many functions to be combined in a method similar to the low-level functional programming language. Moreover, users should know the procedure of query evaluation since the query language is procedural. Kimber [16] have proposed a query language, called HyQ, for the HyTime documents. The HyQ is also a functional query language which is similar to the SGQL. The HyQ provides basic functions for simple queries, and they are combined to generate a complex function. It is also a procedural language. Macleod [20] [21] has defined a query language based on a tree- structured document model. His language has used the concept of path in a document hierarchy. In order to make a structure query, users must know the element names and their hierarchy defined in the DTD. Christophides et al. [8] [9] have extended this path concept and presented a query language, called Extended O_2SQL, which uses path expressions for structure queries. However, their path expression supports only forward directional navigation.

We have extended the path expression to represent backward paths from lower levels to higher levels in the document structure and backward hyperlinks. Thus, users can navigate in either direction freely and select any interested portion of a document or a group of documents. We also have extended the expression to be able to represent the number of hops by a method similar to the regular expression in automata theory. By using our path expression, users can easily control the number of hops of branches or links in the document tree or hypertext graph, and express powerful structure queries. In order to locate ancestors or descendants of an element directly, we also have proposed a novel scheme which uses unique element identifiers(UID's). Thus, we can perform rapid structure query processing by calculation only without disk access.

Much research has been performed to design efficient index structures for database and information retrieval systems [11] [23]. In order to perform structure queries efficiently, index structures that support fast element access must be provided because users want to access all kinds of document elements in the database. However, in the previous systems, little attention has been focused on structured document indexing.

Recently, Sacks-Davis et al. [22] have proposed some possible inverted index structures for structure query processing based on the conventional inverted index structure. The first approach is to maintain the inverted index supporting only document access. That is, the inverted list contains only document identifiers, and no element identifiers. The disadvantage of this approach is that post-processing is required to locate document elements after identifying documents. The cost of the post-processing is considerable if the number of documents to be retrieved is large.

The second approach is to maintain a separate index for each element type. However, the index term should appear in every index causing considerable space overhead. In order to reduce the duplication of index terms, a single combined vocabulary with a separate inverted list for each element type per index term can be used. However, the storage overhead of the inverted list caused by the element identifiers is still great.

Finally, they have proposed a new scheme, called the element locator scheme, for document structure indexing. In this approach, each index term in the inverted list is associated with a path encoding from the root to the leaf and any necessary sibling numbers. This approach also requires considerable storage overhead in the inverted list.

In this paper, we have proposed a new indexing scheme which supports not only processing structure queries efficiently but also reducing the storage overhead of indices considerably. Our scheme exploits the hierarchical document structures and uses the fact that index terms are inherited between hierarchically related elements.

7. Conclusions

Multi-structure information is useful for managing and handling hypermedia documents. The main contribution of this paper is that we propose solutions in modeling, querying, and indexing hypermedia documents in order to fully utilize multi-structure information, while most previous studies have focused on only the logical structure of text-oriented documents.

The document model represents complex hierarchical characteristics of multi-structure information as composite objects, and every structure element is mapped to a type. By using specially designed UID's, we can minimize the storage space for parent-child links and enhance the performance in processing structure queries. Many benefits can be obtained in modeling multimedia data by treating multimedia to contain only position information to BLOB data instead of having the actual data.

Our query language is designed to have advantages in supporting all the query types (i.e., attribute, content, structure, hyperlink query) and all the structures (i.e., logical, spatial/temporal layout, hyperlink network structure). A new index scheme has been developed to reduce the storage overhead and to access document elements efficiently. Its benefits can be maximized by exploiting multi-structure information to optimize the indices.

The document data model and query language presented in this paper are independent of any document standard or a specific DBMS implementation. Thus, the model and language can be implemented in any OODBMS since they are specified in compliance with the ODMG-93 standard.

The index structure suggested in this paper supports boolean queries only. Ranked queries can be supported by associating a weight value with each element identifier in the inverted list. Developing a weighting function for our indexing scheme is planned in future work.

In this paper, we have assumed that the documents in the hypermedia network are static documents. However, documents can change over time. In this case, we have to maintain several versions of a document. Currently, we are studying the versioning issues of hypermedia documents.

The query language in this paper is for searching the hypermedia network. We have not considered the problem of creating a new hypermedia document using the documents in the hypermedia network. We can extend our query language in order to support the functionality of hypermedia document composition.

Acknowledgments

We would like to thank Seong-Joon Yoo and Kyoungro Yoon for their comments and many suggestions.

References

1. J. F. Allen, "Maintaining Knowledge about Temporal Intervals," Comm. of the ACM, Vol. 26, 1983.
2. T. Arnold-Moore, et al., "The ELF Data Model and SGQL Query Language for Structured Document Databases," TR 94-13, CITRI, Australia, 1994.
3. E. Bertino, F. Rabitti, and S. Gibbs, "Query Processing in a Multimedia Document System," ACM Transactions on Office Information Systems, Vol. 6, 1988.
4. G. E. Blake, et al., "Text/Relational Database Management Systems: Harmonizing SQL and SGML," in Proc. of the International Conference on Applications of Databases, 1994.
5. K. Boehm and K. Aberer, "Storing HyTime Documents in an Object-Oriented Database," in Proc. of CIKM'94, 1994.
6. R. G. G. Cattel, et al. ed., The Object Database Standard: ODMG-93, Morgan Kaufmann Publishers, 1994.
7. D. M. Choy, et al., "Document Management and Handling," IEEE '87 Office Automation Symposium, 1987.
8. V. Christophides, et al., "From Structured Documents to Novel Query Facilities," in Proc. of the ACM SIGMOD Conference, 1994.
9. V. Christophides and A. Rizk, "Querying Structured Documents with Hypertext Links using OODBMS," in Proc. of the European Conference on Hypermedia Technology, 1994.
10. C. Faloutsos, "Access Methods for Text," ACM Computing Surveys, Vol. 17, 1985.
11. W. B. Frankes and R. Baeza-Yates ed., Information retrieval: Data Structures and Algorithms, Prentice Hall, 1992.
12. S. J. Gibbs and D. C. Tsichritzis, Multimedia Programming: Object, Environments, and Frameworks, Addison-Wesley, 1995.
13. "ISO 8613. Information Processing - Text and Office Systems - Office Document Architecture (ODA) and Interchange Format," International Organization for Standardization, 1993.
14. "ISO 8879. Information Processing - Text and Office Systems - Standard Generalized Markup Language (SGML)," International Organization for Standardization, 1986.
15. "ISO/IEC 10744. Information Technology - Hypermedia/Time-Based Structuring Language (HyTime)," International Organization for Standardization, 1992.
16. W. E. Kimber, "HyTime and SGML: Understanding the HyTime HyQ Query Language," Available via anonymous ftp at ftp.ifi.uio.no /pub/SGML/HyTime, August 1993.
17. Kyuchul Lee, et al., "Temporal Specification and Synchronization for Multimedia Database Queries," in Proc. of the Int'l Symposium on Next Generation Database Systems and Their Applications, 1993.
18. Y. K. Lee, S. -J. Yoo, K. Yoon, and P. B. Berra, "Querying Structured Hyperdocuments," in Proc. of the 29th Hawaii Int'l Conf. on System Sciences, 1996.
19. Y. K. Lee, S. -J. Yoo, K. Yoon, and P. B. Berra, "Index Structures for Structured Documents," in Proc. of the First ACM Int'l Conf. on Digital Libraries, 1996.
20. I. A. Macleod, "Storage and Retrieval of Structured Documents," Information Processing and Management, Vol. 26, 1990.
21. I. A. Macleod, "A Query Language for Retrieving Information from Hierarchical Text Structures," The Computer Journal, Vol. 34, 1991.
22. R. Sacks-Davis, T. Arnold-Moore, and J. Zobel, "Database Systems for Structured Documents," in Proc. of the International Symposium on Advanced Database Technologies and Their Integration (ADTI '94), 1994.
23. G. Salton and M. J. McGill, Introduction to Modern Information Retrieval, McGraw-Hill, 1983.

Kyuchul Lee is an Associate Professor in the Department of Computer Engineering at Chungnam National University, Taejon, Korea. He received his B.E., M.E., and Ph.D. degrees in Computer Engineering from Seoul National University in 1984, 1986, and 1996, respectively.
In 1994, he worked as a visiting researcher at the IBM Almaden Research Center, San Jose, California. From 1995 to 1996, he worked as a Visiting Professor at the CASE Center at Syracuse University, Syracuse, New York.
His current research areas include Multimedia Database Systems, Hypermedia Systems, Object-Oriented Systems, and Digital Libraries. He has published over 50 technical articles in various journals and conferences. He is a member of ACM, IEEE Computer Society, and Korea Information Science Society.

Yong Kyu Lee is a Senior Member of the Technical Staff of Research and Development Group at Korea Telecom, Seoul, Korea.
He received the B.S. degree in Computer Science from Dongguk University, Seoul, Korea, in 1986, the M.S. degree in Computer Science from Korea Advanced Institute of Science and Technology (KAIST), Taejon, Korea, in 1988, and the Ph.D. degree in Computer and Information Science from Syracuse University in 1996.
From 1988 to 1993, he worked as a Senior Research, Project Leader, and Head of Computer Systems section at the Institute for Defense Information Systems, Seoul, Korea.
His research interests include Hypermedia Systems, Multimedia Information Systems, Digital Libraries, Database Systems, and Software Engineering.

P. Bruce Berra is a Research Professor of Electrical Engineering and Computer Science at Syracuse University, Prior to July 1, 1996, he was the Director of the New York Center for Advanced Technology in Computer Applications and Software Engineering (CASE), Professor of Electrical and Computer Engineering, and a faculty member in Computer and Information Science at Syracuse University. Dr. Berra previously served as Chairman of Industrial Engineering and Operations Research at Syracuse, and has taught at Michigan University, Dearbon campus, Boston University, and Purdue University. His industrial experience includes periods of service with Hughes, Bendix, and IBM. He is currently President of PBB Systems, an AI/database consulting firm.

An IEEE fellow, Dr. Berra has served on the IEEE Computer Society Governing Board, as the editor-in-chief of the Computer Press, on the IEEE Press Editorial Board, and as a member of the Computer Society's Distinguished Visitors Program. He has also served as general chair and program chair of the International Conference on Knowledge and Data Engineering. He has served as an editor for the IEEE Transactions on Knowledge and Data Engineering, IEEE Transactions on Software Engineering, IEEE Transactions on Computers, and as Chairman of the Transactions Advisory Committee. He received his B.S. and M.S. degrees from the University of Michigan and his Ph.D. from Purdue University.

Dr. Berra pursues research interests in Multimedia Information Systems, Parallel Processing for Large Data and Knowledge Bases, and Optical Database Machines. He was recently presented with the L. C. Smith College of Engineering and Computer Science Award for Excellence in Scholarship for contributions to knowledge in his field. In 1994 and 1995, he was a finalist in the Supporter of Entrepreneurship category of Entrepreneur of the Year Institute Awards.

Mutlimedia Tools and Applications, 4, 225–243 (1997)

Techniques for Fast Partitioning of Compressed and Uncompressed Video

DONALD A. ADJEROH, M. C. LEE donald, mclee [@cs.cuhk.edu.hk]
Department of Computer Science and Engineering, The Chinese University of Hong Kong, HONG KONG.

CYRIL U. ORJI orji@fiu.edu
School of Computer Science, Florida International University, Miami, FL 33199, USA.

Abstract. Video partitioning is the segmentation of a video sequence into visually independent partitions, which represent various identifiable scenes in the video. It is an important first step in considering other issues in video databases management, such as indexing and retrieval. As video partitioning is a computationally intensive process, effective management of digital video requires highly efficient techniques for the process. In general, for compressed and uncompressed video, the basic mechanism used to reduce computation is by selective processing of a subpart of the video frames. However, so far the choice of this proportion has been made randomly, without any formal basis. An ad hoc selection of this subpart cannot always guarantee a reduction in computation while ensuring effective partitioning.

This paper presents formal methods for determining the optimal window size and the minimum thresholds which ensure that decisions on scene similarity are made on a reliable, effective and principled basis. Further, we propose the use of neighbourhood-based colour ratios, and derive the ratio feature for both uncompressed and transform coded video. The neighbourhood-based ratio features account for both illumination variation and possible motion in the video, while avoiding the computational burden of explicit motion compensation procedures. Empirical results showing the performance of the proposed techniques are are also presented.

Keywords: video partitioning, video indexing, compressed video, colour ratio features

1. Introduction

Digital video has come to stay as an important and integral part of multimedia information systems. However, the utility of the computer in the manipulation and management of digital video is highly limited by the enormous volumes of data often involved. The primary method currently employed in handling the volume problem involves the use of some video compression techniques. Thus, the majority of video information is stored in compressed form, and some techniques are required to manage video directly in compressed form. The process of video partitioning is an important step in approaching the other problems in video databases management, such as indexing and retrieval. With the huge volumes of data involved (even in compressed form), effective management of digital video requires highly efficient techniques for the partitioning stage.

Video partitioning involves segmenting a video sequence into independent shots which represent various identifiable scenes in the video. It also involves the determination and classification of the various editing effects which may be part of the original video sequence. Most of the approaches so far proposed involve the manipulation of the pixel values at each or selected pixel location in the video frame [9, 13, 25]. The huge volumes of data involved, however, make video partitioning very computationally intensive. More recently, proposals have been made for performing the video partitioning process directly on compressed video, [3, 26, 12], particularly, those based on the Discrete Cosine Transform (DCT). In general, both for compressed and uncompressed video, the basic mechanism used to reduce the amount of computation is by choosing a subpart of the entire frame for processing. However, so far the choice of what proportion of the frame to be processed has been made as a random decision, without any formal basis [13]. It is possible that on the one hand, a random choice may underestimate the proportion of the frame needed to be considered, in which case the chosen blocks/subframes do not provide enough information to discriminate between the video scenes. On the other hand, a random choice may grossly overestimate the proportion of the frame that need to be considered, thereby negating the original objective of complexity reduction. Still, an arbitrary (or even a fixed) choice of the thresholds may not account well for possible variations in the video characteristics, such as frame size, noise, compression ratio, etc.

This paper proposes some techniques for effective partitioning of video sequences, in both compressed and uncompressed domains. We start by presenting formal methods for deciding on the optimal size and number of windows (or subframes) into which the video frames should be divided for the purpose of video partitioning. Then, we determine the minimum threshold (or proportion of the video frame) that must be compared such that, with respect to video scene changes, a decision made on the basis of the minimum proportion will always be the same as (or close to) that made based on the entire video frame. This thus ensures that the decision is not made in an ad hoc manner. For the case of block based transform coded video, we show how the selection can be made based on the block size used to encode the video. To ensure effectiveness of the techniques, without sacrificing efficiency, the use of neighbourhood-based colour ratios is proposed. Then, ratio features for both uncompressed video and transform coded video sequences are derived which account for both illumination variation and possible motion in the video, while avoiding the computational burden of explicit motion compensation procedures.

The paper is organized as follows. Section 2 briefly describes current approaches to video partitioning (for compressed or uncompressed video), and some of the basic schemes for reducing the computational complexity. Next, formal methods to avoid the current ad hoc choice of the window size and thresholds are presented. Section 4 shows how the techniques can be used to partition uncompressed video, while section 5 extends the approach to support video partitioning directly in the compressed domain. Finally, some experimental results are presented and the paper concludes with a discussion of some issues related to the proposed methods.

2. Related Work

Video partitioning (or segmentation) involves the automatic detection of the scene changes in a video sequence. This effectively divides the video into separate partitions, called scenes or shots. To partition the video, each pair of *consecutive frames* is compared to determine frame pairs with significant statistical differences. (We use the term consecutive frames to refer to two frames separated by the chosen temporal skip factor, $\varphi = 1, 2, \ldots$). Using an analogy from automatic indexing and string search in text databases, Nagasaka and

Tanaka [13] proposed methods for automatic video indexing based on differences in colour histogram. The use of colour and the χ^2 test criteria made their approach different from the work of Tonomura [21] which only considered sum of grey level histogram differences. Otsuji and Tonomura, [15] also used image differences by observing that the distribution of frame differences exhibited some high isolated peaks -projections- at the scene boundaries and thus suggested the use of some filters to detect such projections. Practically, these filters correspond to the usual notion of threshold used by most other authors. In a knowledge based approach proposed in [20], objects in the video were identified by comparing pre-defined domain models with key features of the frame as identified by the histogram comparison methods. The applicability of this approach however seems to be limited to such areas as news video, where models of the video content can be available a priori. Hampapur *et al* [9] and Zhang *et al* [25] have provided a more comprehensive view of the video segmentation problem. They also used colour histogram differences, and provided some techniques for automatic threshold selection and detection of gradual scene changes using a multiple-pass strategy. Motion induced changes were avoided using approaches based on optical flow computations.

While most of the above methods chose a subset of the entire frame as a means of reducing the amount of computation, no attempt has been made at providing a formal basis for making such a choice. The problem has been recognized in [24], but no explicit solution was provided. Another problem with existing approaches is that they are often based on mere manipulation of pixel values - neglecting the problem of illumination variation inherent in the video production process [8, 9]. Vrhel and his colleagues [22] have proposed a model for filtering the recording and viewing illuminants, while Nicolas and Labit [14] have recognized the problem and thus proposed a motion and illumination compensated technique in the context of image sequence coding. However, it is the problem of illumination invariant indexing that motivated the use of colour ratios as features for indexing image databases [6, 10]. Thus we build on the work reported in [10] and use neighbourhood based colour ratios to eliminate the effect of illumination changes and motion in the video.

More recently, the high computation and space requirements involved in video partitioning have led to proposals for video partitioning directly on the compressed video. Arman *et al* [3] proposed a method that suggests a possible change of scene if the difference between the dot product of selected DCT coefficients exceeds a given threshold. Arman's method however lacked mechanisms for motion-induced differences, and they did not consider special effects. Zhang *et al* [26] used coefficient differences rather than their dot product. However, they also suggested the use of all the coefficients for a given block, which is analogous to pixel by pixel comparison in the spatial domain. To account for possible motion in the video, they combined the above method with some features based on the motion compensation frames used in MPEG video compression, and equally used the multiple-pass multiple-threshold approach [25] for detecting special effects. The motion compensation strategy is highly dependent on the MPEG based video compression. Moreover, the use of the entire coefficients, and multiple pass strategy may not be attractive for reasons of efficiency. Other recent proposals for compressed domain based partitioning have been reported in [12] where they used only the DC component of the DCT coefficients. Obviously, since the DC component provides an average for pixels in a block, this method may not be robust in the face of highly active scenes.

Generally, the compressed domain based partitioning techniques provide a lot of reduction in computational size, due to the smaller set of features they manipulate. However, like the approaches used for uncompressed video, they generally suffer from the problems of illumination variations, and arbitrary choice of thresholds on the proportion of the frame to consider for scene difference comparison. We use the linearity and stability properties of the colour ratio features [10] and the approaches to transform domain based video compositing [4, 19] to derive motion and illumination invariant ratio features for the transform coded video. We also show how the optimal window size and thresholds can be applied in block based compressed video. Because the major objective is efficient partitioning and classification, the proposed techniques avoid traditional methods such as multiple pass, multiple thresholds [25, 26] due to their inherent computational burden.

3. Optimal Window Size and Thresholds

The idea of choosing only a proportion of the frame is the basic method used to achieve reduction in computational complexity. Usually, the frame is divided into smaller sections, called windows or subframes, and comparison of two adjacent frames is made on a subset of the windows. However, currently, the choice of the window size is often done in an arbitrary fashion, and the subset of the windows for comparison is often chosen at random. Statistically, ad hoc random selection of such parameters can only be effective in about half the time. In this section, we present a principled basis for the selection of the optimal window size for the purpose of efficient video frame comparison. Armed with the optimal window size, we determine the optimal number of windows. To speed up the frame comparison process, we perform premature termination of the comparison process whenever it is clear that further consideration of the remaining windows will make no significant difference to the match result. This means that we must provide a formal method for determining the threshold, or minimum number of windows that must be compared before terminating the match process.

3.1. Optimal Colour Ratio Histogram Matching

In [10], a description of an approach for matching colour ratio histograms was presented. Fast colour ratio histogram matching with premature termination involves matching the histograms in a stepwise incremental fashion, by choosing a step (or group) size for each matching stage. The problem then is how to choose the optimal step size to minimize the number of match steps, and then determine the minimum proportion of the bins that must be matched before prematurely terminating the matching process. Using the occupancy probability model, these parameters were found to be related to the histogram bin size, the allowed probability of error in the match process, and the possible error in the histogram generation process or noise in the image. Here we make use of some of the results. More details including derivations of the formulae used here can be found in [2].

Threshold Selection. Based on the error from the histogram generation process ε, and the allowed probability of random match ρ, the minimum proportion of the total histogram bins b that must be matched to gurantee that match results are not just due to a random occurrence of matching bins is found to be:

$$\hbar_{min} \geq \frac{\log(\rho)}{b \log\left(\frac{1}{1+\frac{4}{\varepsilon b^2}}\right)} \tag{1}$$

Optimal Match Step Size. The optimal match step (or group) size which minimizes the number of match steps is given by

$$z_o = b\left[1 - e^{\frac{1}{b}\ln\left(\frac{1}{2(b+1)}\right)}\right] \tag{2}$$

Optimal Termination Step. Using the above, we can find the optimal termination step, S_{T_o}, as follows: At termination, the number of bins involved in the matching process is given by: $b_o = z_o S_{T_o}$. Then, before terminating the matching process, the condition below should be met:

$$\sum_{i=1}^{b_o} bin[i] \geq \hbar_{min} \tag{3}$$

$bin[i]$ is the bin count at bin location i. If the bins are not sorted, then the sub-optimal termination step, $S_{T_{so}}$, can be obtained before starting the matching process using

$$S_{T_{so}} = \left\lceil \frac{b\hbar_{min}}{z_o} \right\rceil \tag{4}$$

When the bins are sorted, then (4) could obviously over estimate the optimal termination step. Thus with regard to the prevailing error parameters, terminating the matching process at the (sub)optimal termination step ensures that the required minimum proportion of the bins are matched, while avoiding considering the remaining bins which would not have much effect on the match result.

3.2. *Relation to Optimal Window Size and Threshold Selection*

It can be observed that the problem of window size and thresholds in video partitioning can be viewed as analogous to that of matching histogram bins. Considering the entire video frame (i.e. the number of pixels) as the bin size, we can obtain the minimum threshold (or proportion) to be matched. Also, using similar arguments, the optimal window size needed for video partirioning can be viewed as corresponding to the optimal step (or group) size in the case of the histogram. Then, once again we can determine the optimal (or at least sub-optimal) termination step - in this case the optimal number of windows that must be matched before declaring two frames as being similar. However, before the above equations can be applied to video, we have to make certain considerations. For instance, typically, the number of pixels involved in a video frame is far more than the number of typical histogram bins. We present the modified relations below, where, N = frame size in pixels, f_{min} = minimum proportion of the frame that must be compared to avoid random match, ε is a small positive constant and depends on the video characteristic, e.g. the amount of noise, and ρ retains its previous meaning.

Minimum Threshold.

$$f_{min} \geq \frac{\log(\rho)}{\sqrt{N}\log\left(\frac{1}{1+\frac{4}{\varepsilon N}}\right)} \tag{5}$$

Optimal Window Size.

$$W_o = \left[N\left(1 - e^{\frac{1}{N}\ln\left(\frac{1}{2(N+1)}\right)}\right)\right]^2 \tag{6}$$

The dimessions of the optimal window size can easily be computed using W_o. Let the original image be of size $M \times L$, and let M_o and L_o be the corresponding dimesions of the window. Then

$$M_o = \left(\frac{W_o M}{L}\right)^{\frac{1}{2}}; \quad L_o = \left(\frac{W_o L}{M}\right)^{\frac{1}{2}} \tag{7}$$

Optimal Number of Windows.

$$N_o = N/W_o \tag{8}$$

Minimum Number of Windows Required. We can use the equations above to determine the minimum number of windows that must be involved in the frame comparison to avoid random decision on frame similarity. Let N_{min} represent this minimum, while W_i represents the size of window i. Then before termination,

$$\sum_{i=1}^{N_{min}} W_i \geq N f_{min} \tag{9}$$

If we assume that $W_1 = W_2 = \cdots = W_i = W_o$, then we can choose the minimum integer such that

$$N_{min} \geq \frac{N f_{min}}{W_o} = N_o f_{min} \tag{10}$$

Thus

$$N_{min} \geq \frac{\log(\rho)}{N\sqrt{N}\log\left(\frac{1}{1+\frac{4}{\varepsilon N}}\right)\left[1 - e^{\frac{1}{N}\ln\left(\frac{1}{2(N+1)}\right)}\right]^2} \tag{11}$$

Table 1. Variation of f_{min} and N_{min} with ε and ρ for $N = 288 \times 384$

		N_o	f_{min}	N_{min}
$\varepsilon = 0.001$	$\rho = 0.01$	731	0.3897	285
	$\rho = 0.005$	731	0.4484	328
	$\rho = 0.001$	731	0.5846	427
	$\rho = 0.0005$	731	0.6433	470
	$\rho = 0.0001$	731	0.7795	570
$\rho = 0.001$	$\varepsilon = 0.0075$	731	0.4410	324
	$\varepsilon = 0.0005$	731	0.2974	328
	$\varepsilon = 0.0001$	731	0.0673	50

Table 1 and Figures 1 and 2 show the variation of N_o, W_o, f_{min} and N_{min}, with N, ε and ρ.

After obtaining the minimum number of windows that must be compared, the next question is how to choose this subset so as to maximize the coverage over all parts of a given frame. While many issues such as scene activity and adaptability, could be taken into account, efficiency precludes a complicated treatment. Straight forward methods could be to choose the first few windows until the minimum required number of windows are compared. This could be done sequentially, spirally, or even randomly. However a better approach could be to define some criteria, such as minimum distance between the windows, so that by choosing the minimum number of windows as given by (11), subject to the minimum distance criterion, the major changes in the frames can be covered. Also, other information such as how a typical scene varies, say at the frame sides, at the central portion, just randomly, etc. can also be used in deciding which particular windows to choose. Obviously, this is an area that is worth further investigation.

4. Video Partitioning for Uncompressed Video

One major limitation of current approaches in video partitioning arises from their neglect of the relatively obvious problem of illumination changes during the video production process. Consequently, they are often fooled by small changes in illumination across the windows in the frame, or between two frames. Another problem of concern is the possible motion in the video scene, and some strategies have been proposed based on motion vector analysis [25] - which in itself is very time consuming. Funt and Finalyson [6], and Lee and Adjeroh [10] have presented initial results on the effectiveness of colour ratio indexing for image databases. They showed that neighbourhood based colour ratios are invariant under various changes in view condition, including both spectral and intensity variations of the illuminant. Here, we use colour ratios to obtain illumination invariant and motion invariant features for window based video partitioning.

The neighbourhood colour ratios used in [10] can be formulated using a simpler but more general model:

$$\Phi(x,y) = \frac{h(x-1,y) + h(x+1,y) + h(x,y-1) + h(x,y+1)}{4h(x,y)} \tag{12}$$

where $h(x, y)$ is a function of the pixel value at location (x, y) in the image, and the case is for 4-neighbours. The above equation can easily be generalized for any arbitrary number of neighbours. Typically, $h(.)$ has been used as the RGB colour values [10], or a function of their logarithm [6].

In comparing two images, ratio histograms were utilized. However, for the case of window-based video partitioning, the window size is typically too small (see Figure 2) for ratio histogram comparisons to be effective. Moreover, the requirement for fast comparison makes it inexpedient to compute the ratio histograms for each of the selected windows. Thus, a new measure for comparison using the colour ratios is formulated as follows:

$$\Psi(f_n, i) = \prod_{j=1}^{W_i} \Phi_j \tag{13}$$

$$\xi(f_n, f_{n+\varphi,i}) = \frac{\Psi(f_n, i)}{\Psi(f_{n+\varphi}, i)} \tag{14}$$

where $f_n = n^{th}$ frame in the video sequence, φ = temporal skip factor, Φ_j is computed from (12) for the jth pixel location in the window, and W_i = window size for window i. Then we define a window-based frame similarity measure using (15) and use the difference between the $\Im(.)$ values from consecutive frames to check for scene changes.

$$\Im(f_n, f_{n+\varphi}, i) = \begin{cases} 1 - \xi(f_n, f_{n+\varphi}, i) & : \quad \xi(.) \leq 1 \\ & : \\ 1 - \frac{1}{\xi(f_n, f_{n+\varphi}, i)} & : \quad \text{otherwise} \end{cases} \tag{15}$$

It can be observed that the neighbourhood nature of the ratios, and the preservation of local information due to window based comparison ensures motion invariant features, unless the motion between consecutive frames spans beyond the neighbourhood. This is obviously not the case in typical video, and for small values of φ, say less than 10. The general algorithm for partitioning uncompressed video can be summarized as follows:

1. Determine the optimal window size, the optimal number of windows, and the minimum proportion of windows that must be considered.
2. Select the first consecutive frames
   - Compute the neighbourhood ratio at each point in the selected windows
   - Compute the overall ratio feature for each window
   - Compare the ratio features from each window with that of the corresponding window in the next frame
   - Declare scene change between frames if the number of windows with significant difference passes a threshold, or if the average difference based on the selected windows passes a threshold. Otherwise declare no scene change.

3. Take up the next pair, and repeat the procedure.

Step 1 can be performed as a one-off calculation if all the frames have the same size.

5. Video Partitioning for Compressed Video

Video partitioning in the compressed domain usually relies on the inherently smaller amount of data in this domain to achieve high improvement in efficiency. The approach we present is motivated by the linear and stability properties of the colour ratio features. Thus, the approach described below is based on video compressed using linear orthogonal transforms. The ratio distribution is invariant under such transformations. We describe briefly, the concept of transform based video coding and representation, and then show how video partitioning is performed in the compressed domain using neighbourhood ratios.

5.1. Transform Domain Video Representation

By transform domain video representation, we refer to how video information, already in compressed form is represented, the compression being based on some form of transform coding [5]. While transforms on their own provide no compression per se, they expose the correlation between the pixels, and possible redundancies in the original spatial domain. A coding scheme can then take advantage of these facts to store the video information, with possibly a smaller number of bits. Though linear and non linear transforms can be used, most compression schemes are based on one form of linear transform or another, such as KLT, DFT, DCT, etc. Recently, compression schemes based on wavelets and fractals have also been proposed. Although the KLT is considered as the optimal transform (in terms of the ability to pack most of the energy into the fewest coefficients, de-correlation of the inputs and minimization of the mean square error), most standard compression techniques such as JPEG [16, 23], MPEG [7], and H.261 [11] are based on the DCT. This is primarily due to the asymptotic equivalence between the DCT and the KLT, and the existence of fast transforms for the DCT [18]. We thus concentrate on DCT based compressed video, though the proposed techniques can be applied to any linear orthogonal transform.

The 2-dimentional DCT is defined by a pair of equations representing the forward and the inverse transforms respectively. The forward DCT and the inverse DCT are defined by (16) and (17) respectively:

$$H(u,v) = \frac{2C(u)C(v)}{\sqrt{ML}} \sum_{x=0}^{M-1} \sum_{y=0}^{L-1} h(x,y) \cos\frac{(2x+1)u\pi}{2M} \cos\frac{(2y+1)v\pi}{2L} \tag{16}$$

$$h(x,y) = \frac{2}{\sqrt{ML}} \sum_{u=0}^{M-1} \sum_{v=0}^{L-1} H(u,v)C(u)C(v) \cos\frac{(2x+1)u\pi}{2M} \cos\frac{(2y+1)v\pi}{2L} \tag{17}$$

where, $C(p) = \begin{cases} 1/\sqrt{2} & : \; p = 0 \\ 1 & : \; \text{otherwise} \end{cases}$

$h(x, y)$ = 2-D sample value in spatial domain, $H(u, v)$ = 2-D DCT coefficients, and M and L are the block dimensions.

To achieve compression, each coefficient is quantized (using some quantization table) and then encoded using some coding schemes such as Huffman coding or arithmetic coding. To obtain the original data, the process is reversed, - decoding and dequantization, and then performing the inverse DCT on the resulting values using (17) .

The video partitioning scheme described below makes use of the orthogonality and linearity of the transform used to code the video. The distribution of the ratio features is invariant under linear transformations, and thus we can compute equivalent ratio features using the transform coefficients. The partitioning technique is independent of the quantization stage, and therefore can use either the quantized or the dequantized coefficients.

5.2. *Optimal Thresholds for Blocks*

With the data in the compressed domain already divided into blocks, it is simple to apply the discussion of section 3.2 to obtain the optimal thresholds, in terms of the minimum number of blocks that should be compared. Depending on the size of the image, The pre-defined block sizes (block sizes are already fixed by the compression scheme) may however not be the same as the optimal window size. With 8×8 blocks, for a frame size of N, we have :

$$N_{min} \geq \frac{\sqrt{N}\log(\rho)}{64\log\left(\frac{1}{1+\frac{4}{\varepsilon N}}\right)} \tag{18}$$

5.3. *Colour Ratio Features in the Transform Domain*

For the transform domain, the notion of neighbourhoods is used in the context of neighbouring blocks, and not the neighbouring coefficients. This modification is necessary due to the characteristics of the DCT as can be observed from (16) and (17). The neighbouring coefficients in the transform domain may not necessarily be the same even if their spatial domain sample values are. However, for a given (x, y) position in two given blocks with the same sample values in corresponding positions in the spatial domain, if $h(x, y)$ is the same for the two locations, then the corresponding transform coefficients $H(u, v)$ will also be the same.

Smith [19] has provided equivalent methods for performing some spatial domain video compositing functions in the transform domain using the quantized coefficients. In particular, linear scaling and pixel addition were modelled using the following pairs:

$$p(x, y) = \alpha f(x, y); \quad P(u, v) = \alpha\lambda F(u, v) \tag{19}$$

$$p(x, y) = f(x, y) + g(x, y); \quad P(u, v) = \lambda_1 F(u, v) + \lambda_2 G(u, v) \tag{20}$$

with

$$\lambda = \frac{QT_{FT}(u,v)}{QT_{IT}(u,v)} \tag{21}$$

where $f(.)$ and $g(.)$ represent two different images, and $p(.)$ is the result of the manipulation; $F(.)$, $G(.)$ and $P(.)$ are their respective transform domain representations. $QT_{FT}(u,v)$ denotes the value in the quantization table for location (u,v), and $QT_{IT}(u,v)$ represents the corresponding value in the dequantization table. In our case, $f(.)$ and $g(.)$ will actually represent two neighbouring blocks, and for our purpose, we assume $\lambda_1 = \lambda_2 = \lambda$. Though different quantization tables can be used for different blocks as in MPEG, this assumption may not be as restrictive as it appears, since in most applications, the default quantization table is used, in which case $\lambda_1 = \lambda_2$.

Then, the corresponding transform domain equivalent for the neighbourhood ratios defined in (12) can be obtained in terms of the transform coefficients, viz:

$$\Phi(u,v) = \frac{\frac{1}{n}\sum_{i=1}^{i=n} \lambda_i H_i(u,v)}{\lambda H(u,v)} = \frac{\frac{1}{n}\sum_{i=1}^{i=n} H_i(u,v)}{H(u,v)} \tag{22}$$

where n=no of neighbouring blocks involved, $H(u,v)$ is the transform coefficient at location (u,v) for the block under consideration, and $H_i(u,v)$ is the the coefficient at the corresponding (u,v) location in the ith neighbouring block.

Thus the ratio feature is independent of the quantization coefficients. This means that we can equally use the DCT coefficients directly. Since most of the coefficients will be zero, (22) is re-written as :

$$\Phi(u,v) = \begin{cases} \frac{\frac{1}{n}\sum_{i=1}^{i=n} H_i(u,v)}{H(u,v)} & : \quad H(u,v) \neq 0 \\ & : \\ 1 & : \quad \text{otherwise} \end{cases} \tag{23}$$

Then, we obtain the equivalent block-wise ratio feature using (13):

$$\Psi(f_n, i) = \prod_{j=1}^{\eta-1} \Phi_j \tag{24}$$

where $\eta - 1$ is the number of retained AC coefficients, and i represents the block under consideration. The last equation, (24) is computed only for the chosen AC coefficients, since each block still has only one DC ratio feature. Two basic methods can be used in choosing the AC coefficients. One is simply to choose all non zero coefficients, or all those whose magnitute passes a specified threshold. The second is to choose a fraction of the AC coefficients such that the majority of the non- zero coefficients are used. Given the probability density and distribution functions of typical AC coefficient values, to choose the coefficients, we can require that say 90% of their total contribution should be accounted for by the chosen few. Then to accommodate both the DC and AC terms, we compare two blocks using (14) and (15), however with the incorporation of a weighting factor ϕ, $(0 \leq \phi \leq 1)$:

$$\Im(f_n, f_{n+\varphi,i}) = \phi \Im_{DC}(f_n, f_{n+\varphi}, i) + (1-\phi)\Im_{AC}(f_n, f_{n+\varphi}, i) \tag{25}$$

$\Im_{DC}(.)$ and $\Im_{AC}(.)$ are computed from (15) using the respective ratios from the DC and AC terms as given by (23) and (24). A comment on the significance of ϕ is appropriate here. The value of ϕ biases the decision on the scene cut detection to either the DC term or the AC components. Since, the DC and AC coefficients usually carry different types of information about the scene, ϕ can be chosen adaptively, depending on the scene. For instance, while the DC component generally represents an average of the sample values in spatial domain, the AC components provide information on the level of "scene activity" or detail [17]. This information can be used to adaptively choose the value of ϕ when comparing similarity between two frames. Typical settings of ϕ could be:

$\phi = 1$: ignore contribution from AC coefficients,
$\phi = 0$: ignore contribution from the DC term
$\phi = \frac{1}{2}$: treat both AC and DC contributions equally.

6. Preliminary Results

To test the performance of the proposed techniques, we carried out a preliminary experimental investigation on a Sun SPARC workstation using both compressed and uncompressed video. First, we checked the behaviour of the formal thresholds for various values of the frame size and error parameters. Then, we used values determined by the formal thresholds to perform video partitioning. For easier comparison of the results, we present the performance of the ratio based methods for compressed and uncompressed domains using the same video sequence.

6.1. *Optimal Windows and Thresholds*

Table 1 and Figure 1 show the behaviour of the thresholds under variations in frame size, and the error parameters, ρ and ε. It can be observed that f_{min} and N_{min} exhibit expected behaviour. As the allowed probability of random match increases, the threshold on the proportion of the frames required decreases. Conversely, as the error in the video, say due to noise increases, the number of windows needed to be matched also increases. However, the graphs also show that for some combination of the error parameters and frame size, the thresholds can be more than 1. While this is theoretically possible, practically, it could mean that such a combination cannot be supported. Typically, this could indicate that the allowed probability of random match is too small, and cannot be guaranteed under the given level of noise in the video (and vice versa), even if all the windows are involved in the frame comparison process. On the other, it could also indicate a breakdown of the proposed techniques under very large values of the frame size. However, in most practical situations, video frame sizes do not take up such theoretically large values. (Also, see [2] for how this problem can be handled).

The plot of the optimal window size is shown in Figure 2. As the graph indicates, the optimal size for the windows rises steeply initially, and then slowly as the frame size becomes large. The graph shows that at very large values of the frame size, the optimal window size becomes less dependent on the frame size. In practice, the theoretical optimal window size can be adjusted slightly so that the entire frame can be covered without using windows of different dimensions.

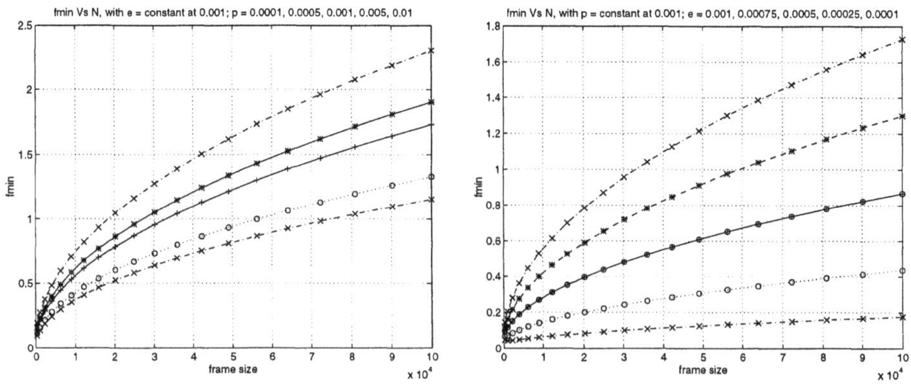

(a) (b)

Figure 1. Variation of f_{min} with ε, ρ and the frame size, N.

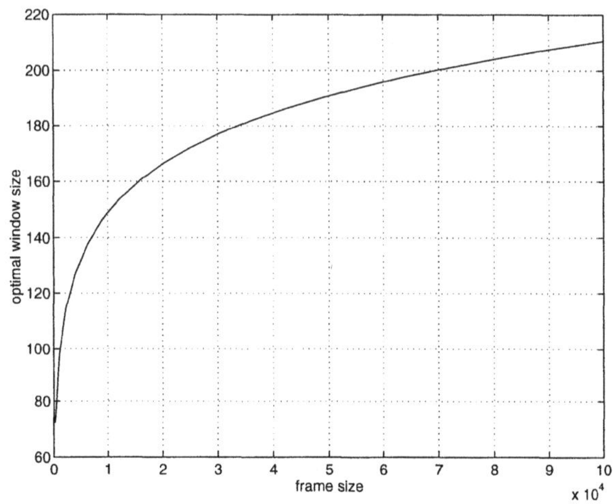

Figure 2. Optimal window size for various values of the frame size

6.2. Partitioning in Compressed and Uncompressed Video

The results on video partitioning are shown in Figures 3 and 4. Figure 3 shows the results of partitioning using uncompressed video, and for different thresholds. To check the effectiveness of the formal thresholds proposed, we compared the original result, when all the windows are used with results for various threshold settings, shown in Table 1. The thresholds are selected based on the error parameters and the frame size as discussed in section 3. The spikes in the figures represent video scene cuts, and it can be seen that the results when using the formal thresholds are almost indistinguishable from the original, when all windows are used.

In Figure 4, the performance of ratio features from the compressed domain is compared with those from the uncompressed domain. The graphs are for 3 settings of the weighting factor: $\phi = \frac{1}{2}, 1, 0$. All the windows are used in both cases, with only 10 coefficients (DC term and 9 AC terms) for the compressed video. As can be seen, the location of the spikes when the transform coefficients are used closely follows the case for uncompressed video. This shows the robustness of the neighbourhood based ratios in the transform domain. It may be stressed that for video partitioning, it is the position of the peaks that is important, and not necessarily their actual peak values, since effective thresholds can be selected for a given feature type, e.g. AC terms, DC terms, their combination, etc. Thus, while for example, AC coefficients generally have smaller peak values than the DC terms, or the uncompressed ratio feature, when compared independently the peaks are always there and appear in the same corresponding position in the video sequence. Also, the closeness with which the frame difference from the AC terms follow that from the uncompressed domain (though with generally lower values), lays more credence to the already mentioned point that the AC terms should not just be ignored in transform based video indexing.

Finally, Table 2 shows the speedup recorded for both compressed and uncompressed domains. The speedup is calculated relative to the time taken using uncompressed video and all the windows (i.e. $f_{min} = 1$). While a modest speedup can be observed for the uncompressed domain, huge speedups are recorded with partitioning using compressed video. The speedup increases with decreasing number of AC coefficients, and thus, as would be expected, using only the DC term provides the highest speedup. Therefore, if efficiency is taken to be more important than reliability of results, only the DC term can be used. On the other hand, it was observed that using only the DC coefficient typically introduces more false alarms, but little or no false dismissals. This could be a welcome phenomena, especially if we are ready to put some more efforts to remove the spurious partitions, introduced due to the limited discriminative ability of the DC coefficient. For this to be attractive, such efforts should be less costly than incorporating a few AC coefficients.

From the preliminary results, the following can be noted: (i) The proposed methods for formal threshold selection work well, and can provide optimal settings for the window size and the proportion of the windows that must be matched before terminating the match. (ii) Neighbourhood based colour ratios are robust and can be used to perform video partitioning in both compressed and uncompressed video. Even at very low thresholds, the ratio feature can still detect the changes in scene. (iii) From (i) an (ii), fast and robust video partitioning can be achieved using formally selected thresholds, and colour ratio based features. For

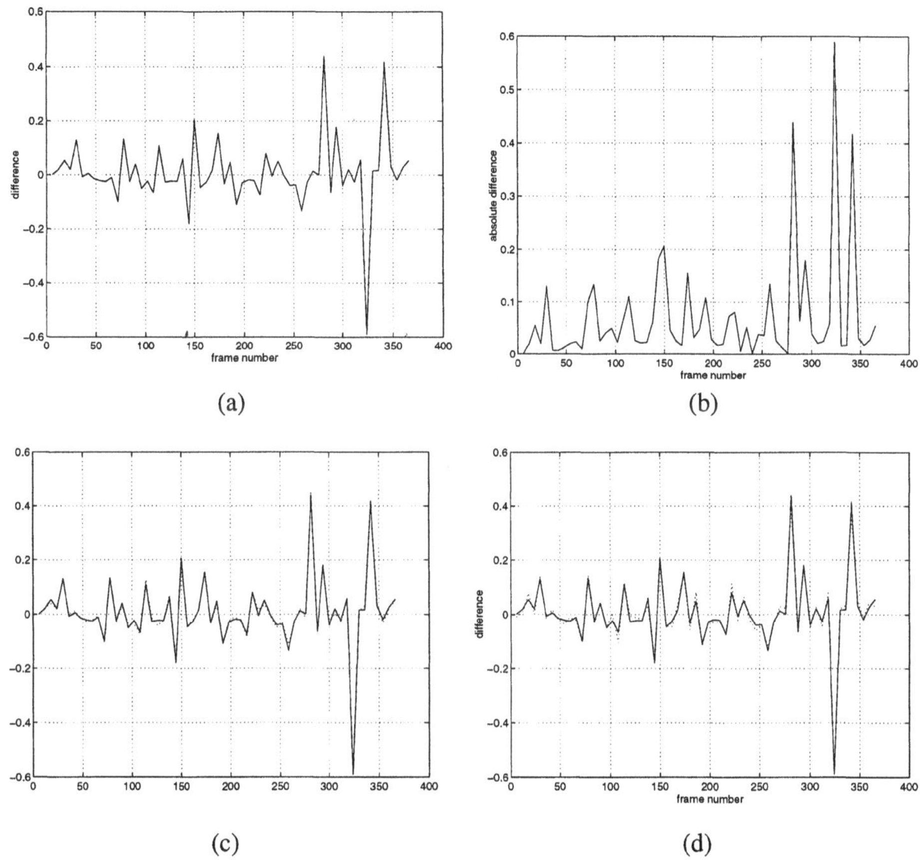

Figure 3. Frame differences for uncompressed video: (a) f_{min}=1 (all windows used); (b) absolute difference for (a); (c) f_{min}=0.5846; (d) f_{min}=0.2974. In (c) and (d), — $f_{min} = 1$; $\cdots$ partitioning using corresponding f_{min}

example, for partitioning in the transform domain, depending on the error parameters, with as little as 30% of the entire frame, and only about 10% of the AC components used, a huge improvement in efficiency can easily be achieved. And most importantly, the results will still be robust and reliable - of course within the limits of the error parameters.

7. Discussion and Conclusion

The paper has argued strongly for a principled approach for the partitioning of video frames into subframes, and the subsequent selection of a subset of the subframes for the purpose

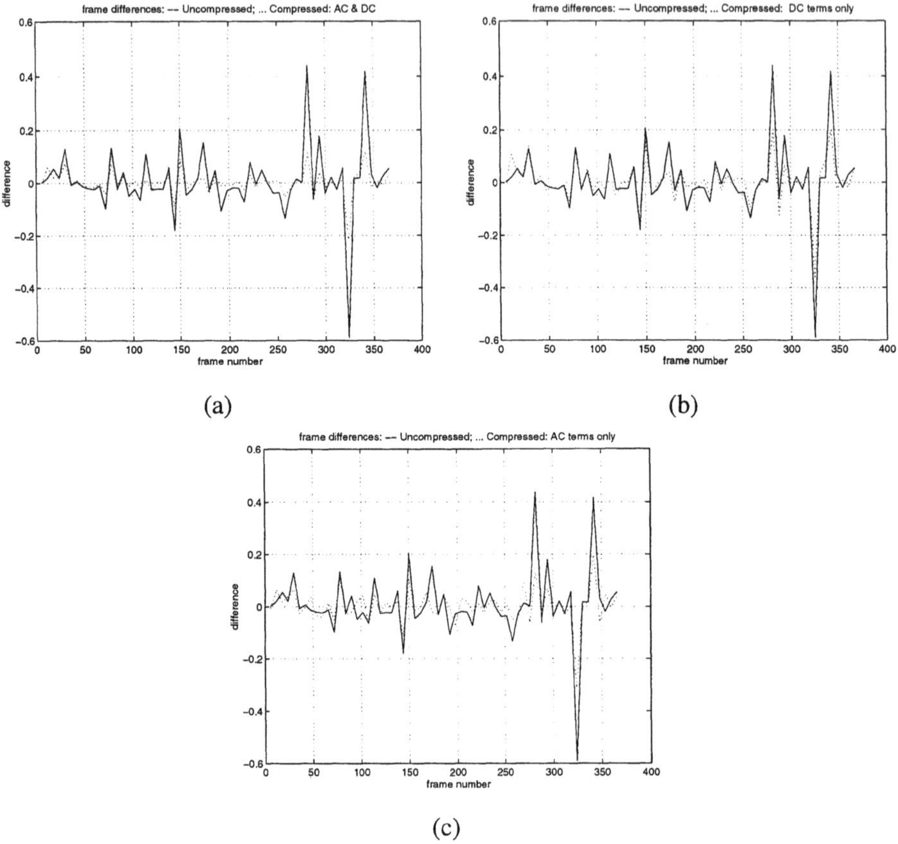

Figure 4. Frame differences from uncompressed video compared with those from compressed video, $f_{min} = 1$ in all cases

of frame comparison. It has provided methods for determining the optimal window sizes and thresholds with respect to minimization of the amount of computation required, and the minimal proportion of the frame that must be compared to ensure that the decisions on scene change (or otherwise) between frames are made on a formal basis rather than the current ad hoc approach. A number of issues can still be raised: for example, whether the computed figures should be the same for all scenes, how best to choose the actual windows to make up the minimal proportion, etc. Some of these are still open questions that have to be resolved. However, the error parameter, ε can provide us with some form of adaptivity based on the video characteristics. For instance, it can be chosen based on the noise in the video, the possible error in the video capture, and for compressed video can be related to the signal to noise ratio due to the compression scheme used. The paper also presented a video partitioning

Table 2. Speedup for partitioning of compressed and uncompresed video (η =no of retained coefficients, including DC term)

f_{min}	DC only	$\eta = 6$	$\eta = 10$	Uncompressed
1.0000	40.4687	8.9310	3.7106	1.0000
0.7795	43.1667	11.1638	4.6250	1.2610
0.5846	61.6667	14.3889	6.2864	1.6796
0.2974	71.9444	23.5455	11.4602	3.2134
0.1537	86.3333	41.7742	20.5556	7.0233
0.0673	68.1579	76.1765	35.9722	15.3099

technique using colour ratios, based on neighbourhood considerations, which eliminates the problems of illumination variation and expensive motion-related computations. New ratio features were also obtained for uncompressed video, and for transform-based compressed video. Further investigation is needed to see how the ratio approach can be extended to other compression schemes, such as those based on wavelets and fractals.

While a number of transform domain based methods seem to neglect the use of the AC coefficients, we have made it an integral part of the comparison. In the transform domain, the AC components can be quite useful in the detection of the level of scene activity. This can be used in selecting the key frames directly in the transform domain. Though the problem of key frame selection (or at least an effective representation of the video sequence) is a necessity for the support of efficient low level search for objects in a video scene, only very few proposals [1, 26] have been made so far. The AC components can be manipulated to provide features for selecting representative frames from the compressed video. Notwithstanding the usefulness of the AC terms, the results also show that where reliability of results can be traded for efficiency, video partitioning can be performed using only the DC coefficients.

The presented techniques achieve fast video partitioning by: (i) partitioning the frame into the optimal number of windows that minimizes the number of comparisons required; (ii) premature termination of the matching process based on the formal minimum thresholds and whenever it is clear that further matching cannot make any significant difference to the results; (iii) performing the partitioning in the compressed domain, where only a fraction of the coefficients are used, and the features can operate on both quantized and dequantized coefficients. Experimental results show that the proposed techniques are effective, and also provide significant improvements in efficiency for the video partitioning process, both in the spatial uncompressed domain and in the transform compressed domain.

References

1. D.A. Adjeroh and M.C. Lee, "Mechanisms for automatic extraction of primary features for video indexing," In, Chin et al. (eds.), Lecture Notes in Computer Science: Image Analysis Applications and Computer Graphics, Springer- Verlag: Berlin-Heildelberg, 1995.
2. D.A. Adjeroh and M.C. Lee, "Probabilistic similarity evaluation using fast incremental matching with optimal premature termination," *Submitted.*

3. F. Arman, A. Hsu, and M-Y Chiu, "Image processing on encoded video sequences," Multimedia Systems, Vol. 1, pp. 211-219, 1994.
4. S-F Chang and D. G. Messerschmitt, "Manipulation and compositing of MC-DCT compressed video," IEEE Journal of Selected Areas in Communication, Vol. 13, pp. 1-11, 1994.
5. R.J. Clarke, Transform Coding of Images, Academic Press, London, 1985.
6. B.V. Funt and G.D. Finlayson, "Color constant color indexing," IEEE Transactions on Pattern Analysis and Machine Intelligence, Vol. 17, pp. 522-529, 1995.
7. D. LeGall, "MPEG: A video compression standard for multimedia applications," Communications of the ACM, Vol. 34, pp. 46-58, 1991.
8. L.S. Gross and L. W. Ward, Electronic Moviemaking, Wadsworth Publishing Co.: Belmont, California, 1994.
9. A. Hampapur, R. Jain and T. E. Weymouth, "Production model based digital video segmentation," Multimedia Tools and Applications: An International Journal, Vol. 1, pp. 9-46, 1995.
10. M.C. Lee and D. A Adjeroh, "Indexing and retrieval in visual databases via colour ratio histograms," in Proceedings, 1st International Conference on Visual Information Systems, Melbourne Australia, 1996, pp. 309-316.
11. M. Liou, "Overview of the px64 kbits/s video coding standard," Communications of the ACM, Vol. 34, pp. 59-63, 1991.
12. J. Meng, Y. Juan and S-F Chang, "Scene change detection in a MPEG compressed video sequence," in Proceedings, IS&T/SPIE Conference on Digital Video Compression and Algorithms, pp. 14-25, 1995.
13. A. Nagasaka, and Y. Tanaka, "Automatic video indexing and full-video search for object appearances," In, E. Knuth, and L.M Wegner (eds.), Visual Database Systems II, Elsevier Science Publishers, pp. 113-127, 1992.
14. H. Nicolas and L. Labit, "Motion and illumination variation estimation using a hierarchy of models: application to image sequence coding," Journal of Visual Communication and Image Representation, Vol. 6, pp. 303-316, 1995.
15. K. Otsuji, and Y. Tonomura, "Projection- detecting filter for video cut detection," Multimedia Systems, Vol. 1, pp. 205-210, 1994.
16. W.B. Pennebaker and J.L Mitchell, JPEG Still Image Data Compression Standard, Van Nostrad Reinhold: New York, 1993.
17. R. Polana and R. Nelson, "Detecting activities," Journal of Visual Communication and Image Representation, Vol. 5, pp. 172-180, 1994.
18. K.R. Rao and P. Yip, Discrete Cosine Transform: Algorithms, Advantages, Applications, Academic Press Inc.: Boston, 1990.
19. B.C. Smith and L. A Rowe, "Algorithms for manipulating compressed images," IEEE Computer Graphics and Applications, Vol. 13, pp. 34-42, 1993.
20. D. Swanberg, C-F Shu, and R. Jain, "Knowledge guided parsing of video databases," in Proceecdings, IS&T/SPIE Symposium on Electronic Imaging Science and Technology (Storage and Retrieval for Image and Video Databases II), San Jose, California, pp. 13-24, 1993.
21. Y. Tonomura, "Video handling based on structured information for hypermedia systems," in Proceedings, International Conference on Multimedia Information Systems, Singapore, 1991 pp. 333-344.
22. M.J. Vrhel, H.J. Trussell, and J. Bosch, "Design and realization of optimal color filters for multi-illuminant color correction," Journal of Electronic Imaging, Vol. 4, pp. 6-14, 1995.
23. G. K. Wallace, "The JPEG still picture compression standard," Communications of the ACM, Vol. 34, pp. 31-44, 1991.
24. W. Xiong, J. C-M Lee, M-C Ip, "Net comparison: a fast and effective method for classifying image sequences," in Proceedings, IS&T/SPIE Conference on Storage and Retrieval for Image and Video Databases III, 1995, pp. 318-28.
25. H-J Zhang, A. Kankanhilli, A. and S.W Smoliar, "Automatic partitioning of full-motion video," Multimedia Systems, Vol. 1, pp. 10-28, 1993.
26. H-J Zhang, L.C. Yong, S. W. Smoliar, "Video partitioning and browsing using compressed data," Multimedia Tools and Applications: An International Journal, Vol. 1, pp. 91-111, 1995.

Don A. Adjeroh holds a BEng degree (*First Class Honours*) in Electronics and Computer Engineering, obtained in 1990, and an MSc in Computer Engineering, obtained in 1994. He is currently completing studies for the Ph.D. degree in the Department of Computer Science and Engineering at The Chinese University of Hong Kong. His current research focus is on Indexing and Retrieval of Visually-stimulated Information, and his general research interests are in Video Processing, Computational aspects of Vision, Distributed Multimedia Systems, Digital Libraries, and Knowledge-based Systems.

M. C. Lee received his PhD degree in Computer Science in 1989 from University of London. He is currently an Associate Professor at the Department of Computer Science and Engineering of The Chinese University of Hong Kong. His current research interests lie in the areas of Image Databases, Video Compression, Multimedia Authoring Systems, AI and Education.

Cyril U. Orji received a Ph.D. degree in Computer Science in 1991 from the University of Illinois, Chicago. He is currently an Assistant Professor in the School of Computer Science at Florida International University, Miami. Previously Dr. Orji was a Member of the Technical Staff at Argonne National Laboratory, Argonne, Illinois. His major research interests are in High Performance I/O Systems, Multimedia Systems, Database and Distributed Computing Systems. Dr. Orji is a member of the Association of Computing Machinery (ACM), and the Institute of Electrical and Electronics Engineers (IEEE).

MIX
Papier aus verantwortungsvollen Quellen
Paper from responsible sources
FSC® C105338
FSC
www.fsc.org

If you have any concerns about our products,
you can contact us on
ProductSafety@springernature.com

In case Publisher is established outside the EU,
the EU authorized representative is:
Springer Nature Customer Service Center GmbH
Europaplatz 3, 69115 Heidelberg, Germany

Printed by Libri Plureos GmbH
in Hamburg, Germany